Go beyond addictions to freedom in Jesus Christ!

Beyond Addictions examines the Biblical basis for issues of addiction. It is designed for personal use or in small groups or as a resource to help deliver men and women from addictive thinking and actions.

Do you want to be free? The truths and profound principles in this book will pave the path for anyone to get beyond their addictions—permanently.

God used my two and a half years in prison to change my life, to help me 'apply' scripture and become a follower of Christ who hears and obeys. This course was instrumental in transforming my thinking and my behavior. God used it to set me free in prison and to keep me free now that I'm on the outside.

After re-reading the *Beyond Addictions* book, I realized how much of it I have incorporated into my daily life since my release two years ago. I heartily recommend it for anyone who truly wants to move beyond all addictions into a free and meaningful life.

John Whitehead, *Beyond Addictions* Graduate 2007

While serving as facility head of Dan River Prison Work Farm from 2003 to 2010 it was my pleasure to observe the development of certain inmates involved with the *Beyond Addictions* study. The men routinely made the transition with biblical values into their daily practices, and carried the training forward. I received visits, calls and notes from released inmates who had participated in the program, and wanted to share success stories with me. The life choices taught and exampled in *Beyond Addictions* freed the men in many different ways.

George Solomon, Regional Director, NC Dept. of Corrections

Beyond Addictions is very important to inmates in the Denton County, TX jail. I have presented it to men at a Pre-Trial Facility and watched God work as they complete lessons. It's a blessing to see men share with new inmates how much this course means to them. I'm hearing from inmates I haven't met who'd like to take the course by mail.

Tom M., Outreach Ministries, Crossroads Bible Church in Double Oak, TX

Anything we put before the true and living God becomes our god. When men realize that this is sin, they come to a point of repentance and begin true healing. B*eyond Addictions* provides a Biblical basis for real life-change based upon true healing. I have seen men take their focus off of themselves and their addictions, and begin to focus on God who is able to deliver them as they apply the messages in this book. Marriages have been reconciled, families have been reunited and men reemerge into the work force.

Tim Fontaine, North Carolina State Elder, Bikers for Christ

Beyond Addictions

Free To Live a New Life in Christ Jesus

By

Jeff Rudd

Big Mac Publishers, Sylacauga, Alabama 35151
Printed and bound in the United States of America

i

Author: Jeff Rudd
Editor: Allison Rudd
Editor   Greg Bilbo
Interior Photos   Marty Allen
Cover Illustration, design © 2011   Jeff Rudd and Greg Bilbo
Cover Photos   IStockPhoto.com/Simone Becchetti

All Scripture quotations are from:
The Holy Bible, New King James Version © 1982 by Thomas Nelson, Inc. Used by permission.

Library of Congress Control Number: 2011933179
Library of Congress Classification Suggestions

1. Addicts -- Rehabilitation
2. Substance abuse – Religious aspects -- Christianity
3. Substance abuse -- Treatment

BISAC / BASIC Classification Suggestions:

1. SEL026000   Self-Help / Substance Abuse & Addiction / General
2. OCC011020   Body, Mind & Spirit / Healing / Prayer & Spiritual
3. SEL013000   Self-Help / Substance Abuse & Addiction / Drug Dependence
4. SEL006000   Self-Help / Substance Abuse & Addiction / Alcoholism
5. OCC011000   Body, Mind & Spirit / Healing / General

ISBN-13: 978-0-9831983-8-3   V 1.0

Big Mac Publisher Book Titles may be purchased in bulk (3 or more) at great discounts for almost any reason including retail purposes and by **retail vendors**, or for educational, business, fund-raising, spiritual or sales promotional. Contact info at Big Mac Publisher's website. http://www.bigmacpublishers.com or contact the author at: freeinchrist@esinc.net

TABLE OF CONTENTS

PART I

WHERE TO START?

Preface
Beginning at the Beginning
Transforming the Way We Think

Prison can be a pretty dark place, but even here, the light of Jesus Christ is changing lives as men and women learn to walk in Christ. Jesus came to set you free. There is no place so dark that Jesus cannot reach, or any life so lost that He cannot save.

Preface

Life and hope, that is what *Beyond Addictions* is about. Jesus came so that you and I could have life, and that more abundantly (John 10:10). We have a living hope in Christ, an assurance, confidence, and expectation of new life in Him now and forever. The hope that we have in Jesus is certain – He loves you and me today; He is returning for us again; we have an eternal home with Him in heaven. As believers in Jesus, these are things that we can be confident in.

What does this have to do with the struggle against addiction? I'll answer that question with one example of new life that was born out of this struggle. Let me tell you a little about Ron. His father committed suicide when he was 13 years old. That was about the time that he started using drugs, and he remained addicted for almost 30 years. Ron is one of the guys who cost us hundreds of thousands of dollars to house in the prison system. He has been convicted of 63 felonies and has spent 18 of the past 26 years in prison. His current sentence began eight years ago. During the first five of those years, he was disciplined for infractions eleven times; seven of those infractions were for "substance possession." You could say that he was a poster-child for the failure of the criminal justice system to rehabilitate. Even though he had gone through many programs, Ron had no hope and no real plans for change. Then something happened, his infractions suddenly stopped; he was a different man and everyone around him could see it. For the past two years he has lived with a sense of hope and freedom, and he has been a model inmate in the prison system. What happened?

In January of 2009, Ron committed his life to Christ. He began reading the Bible and applying it to his life. He took his new faith seriously, and he began to discover that living, breathing, daily faith in Jesus Christ could set him free from his bondage to drug addiction. Ron told me once, "I'm not in prison anymore. I may be surrounded by a wire fence, but I'm free for the first time in my life." That is why he doesn't need drugs to get him through the day. He has a new life. He is free in Christ … in prison.

There is a beautiful passage in the eighth chapter of John where Jesus says, *If the Son therefore shall make you free, you shall be free indeed.* That is what Ron and many other men have experienced. They have applied the lessons learned through *Beyond Addictions* and they are free in Christ, even while serving time. Wouldn't you like to be free?

The *Beyond Addictions* material has been taught in the Guides for Living Course since the fall of 2002. Hundreds of men have graduated and are living as free men in Christ.

The rate at which men are likely to return to prison is called the "recidivism rate." According to the United States Bureau of Justice Statistics, the recidivism rate for all inmates who have been out of prison for at least three years is 51.8%.[1] The recidivism rate for *Beyond Addictions* graduates who have been out of prison for three years or more is 26.4%. So, men who graduate from this course are far less likely to return to prison or to become involved in criminal activity. Most are leading totally different lives as productive citizens, holding down jobs, taking care of their families, and serving in their local churches.

Why are *Beyond Addiction*s graduates less likely to return to prison? There may be a number of reasons. For one, they are motivated to change, and they are willing to accept a Biblical solution to their problems. More importantly, through the course, they are discipled in their relationship with God to go beyond addictions to live a new life in Jesus Christ. As a result, they experience the hope and freedom that God desires for all of us to enjoy.

II Corinthians 5:17 teaches us that if anyone is truly living in Christ, then he or she is a new creation; old things are passed away and all things become new. Addiction is one of the old things that can be removed from the life of a person who is living as a Christian and walking according to the direction of the Holy Spirit.

You may wonder if the Bible really addresses addiction. The answer is absolutely, yes, and thank the Lord. The Bible addresses all forms of addiction, whether your problem is heroine, crack cocaine, alcohol, pornography, sexual addiction or anything else.

The truth of the matter is that most people struggle with some sort of addictive problem. The illegal ones like methamphetamines, crack, pot or other drugs get most of the attention, but the legal, more socially acceptable ones ruin lives just as much. The devil has been tempting

---

[1] U.S. Department of Justice, "Recidivism of Prisoners Released in 1994," 2002 study.

people with sexual lust and alcohol, and using these tools to destroy families since Adam and Eve left the Garden of Eden. In our culture, he also uses addiction to entertainment and material wealth pretty effectively too. John 10:10 reminds us that the thief came to steal, kill and to destroy, and addictive habits are some of his most crafty tools.

This book was written to set you free from addiction. Many good books have been written to explain the problem or to increase your knowledge of addiction. We have tried to make this one a practical guide to applying God's Word to the problem and being set free. You will learn the same lessons that are taught in the *Beyond Addictions* course. Put these lessons to work and you can break the chains that have kept you in bondage. I encourage you to read each chapter as a single lesson and discuss what you are learning with another Christian. Use it as a small-group study or as the basis for a recovery ministry in your church. Underline the points that directly address your life, and by all means, apply it. As the Holy Spirit teaches you, you will be inspired to share this message with others who can benefit from living free in Jesus Christ too.

You can download MP3 audio or podcasts of the *Beyond Addictions* classes as it is taught in prison on the Free In Christ Prison Ministries website http://ficpm.com/gba.php. You can also download full-page copies of the course assignments at the same location.

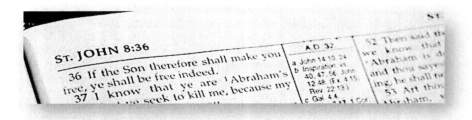

"When we put Christ first and give our heart to Him to do His will, we are free. He holds the key to our salvation and our healing."

-    W.B. (*Beyond Addictions* Graduate 2010)

Prepare to be set free.

Beginning at the Beginning

Chapter 1

Temptations are an appeal to meet righteous needs in an
unrighteous way. ... God has a righteous way to meet the
longing that your temptation has stirred.
Bill Thrasher, *A Journey to Victorious Praying*

Addictions have ruined millions, possibly billions, of lives and
devastated families for centuries. The headlines are filled with stories
of alcoholism, drug addiction, sexual addictions and other ugly pictures
of lives derailed by these miserable problems.

One story reads, "*Alcoholic is accused of incestuous relationship
with two daughters.* A once prominent leader of a local city has been
cited for engaging in sexual relationships with both of his daughters.
According to sources, he was drunk at the time of each encounter."

Another says, "*National leader caught in web of sexual addiction
ruins life and career.* Law & order judge is captured during sexual es-
capade and is being held without bond in a local jail. Further investiga-
tion has turned up evidence of previous instances where he visited
known prostitutes and used his office to commit crimes including arson
and possibly murder. Authorities are investigating possible connections
with the deaths of his first wife and father-in-law which occurred twenty years earlier."

These stories could have appeared in your local newspaper. The
truth is that both factual accounts occurred more than 3,000 years ago
and are told in the Bible. The first story regards the sad conclusion of
Lot's life. A formerly wealthy and prominent land and cattle owner, he
also served as a leader in the city of Sodom. Allowing his life to be influenced by the sinful culture in the city, he lost everything including
his wife and the respect of his daughters. His story is told in the nine-
teenth chapter of the book of Genesis.

The second headline deals with the life of Samson, one of the most
gifted men to serve Israel during the two hundred year period that judges ruled the nation from 1250-1050 BC. He allowed his own physical

appetites to enslave him. In this way, he was no different from the modern day businessman or politician who is addicted to cocaine or alcohol. They wake every morning thinking of ways to satisfy their craving, all the while appearing to live normal lives.

The battle against addiction is not new. Neither is the method of victory. Remarkably, the New Testament records that Lot and Samson were forgiven and redeemed. In fact, both are included in the "hall of faith" in the eleventh chapter of the book of Hebrews. Here is some good news: Jesus Christ can forgive and redeem you too. Regardless of the depths of your problems or the length of your addiction, Jesus Christ can rescue you and give you a new life.

Let's look at one more headline. *"Local woman miraculously delivered from years of abuse.* Disrespected by the people in her small town, she was infamous for her relationships with many men. Married five times, she was now living with her boyfriend when someone stepped into her world and changed her life."

This story of the woman at the well outside of Samaria is told in the fourth chapter of the Book of John. It appears that she was entrapped by her emotional or physical needs. Maybe she had been abused as a child, or she may have thought that the only way she could find any security or acceptance was through sexual relationships with the men in her life. After that, it became easy to slip from one relationship to another, to believe that this was the best that she could do or that life would always be that way.

Who was the caring man who changed her life? His name is Jesus. The good news is that Jesus is still in the business of setting people free from bondage to addiction.

Maybe you have been in church all of your life and thought that addiction to Internet pornography could never happen to you … but it did. Or maybe you have tried every form of rehabilitation only to slip back into drug use after a while. Let me share a little hope. You are not alone, the problem is not new, and Jesus still has a plan for your life. He wants to forgive you and restore you. He offers you a hope and a future (Jeremiah 29:11).

Going Back to the Foundation

In order to solve the problem of addiction, we need to rebuild from the ground up. We need to see this problem for what it is, remove it and allow the Lord to rebuild our lives.

Addictions are an awful intrusion into lives that God created for a purpose. They are cancerous sins that can grab hold of you and eat at your very soul. They are common problems with Christians, and epidemic among non-Christians.

For example, at the time of this printing, statistics indicate that more than one-half of all illegal drug use is related to the improper use of prescription pain medication. Many of the people who have fallen to this type of addiction are suburban professionals. Many attend church each week. So drug addiction isn't restricted to the poor and homeless; it hits families on both sides of the tracks inside and outside of church buildings. This has long been the case with alcoholism too. It doesn't matter if you are addicted to beer, cheap whiskey or expensive scotch, addiction is addiction and it will ruin your life.

Drugs and alcohol aren't the only problems; in fact, they probably aren't the biggest problems. Millions of Christian and non-Christian men are caught in the web of Internet pornography. They have bought the lie that "stolen waters are sweet and bread eaten in secret is pleasant" as it is described in Proverbs 9:17. They are hiding their secret addiction to pictures on the computer just like a drug addict buries his stash in the backyard. This scheme of Satan has probably ruined as many families and affected as many lives as drugs and alcohol combined. Addiction to porn is just a more subtle form of poison than dope or booze.

We could talk about the problem all day, but we want to focus on the solution. The addiction that you have struggled with may seem to have overwhelming power but there is a greater power in the world and He came to set you free. Praise God that we can get beyond the addiction through our relationship with Jesus Christ.

We are impacted more by our closest personal relationships than by any other influence in our lives. The people you spend time with affect the way you think, your opinions on various topics, your greatest interests and your actions. You are radically influenced by the people you hang around. In fact, involving yourself with positive role models will separate you from negative influences.

This is also true regarding your relationship with Jesus. The more time you spend with Jesus, the greater impact He has on you, and the more like Him you become. The more you are separated *unto* Jesus, the more you are separated *from* addictions, and the less likely you are to go back to them. So, throughout this book, we are going to focus on Jesus Christ. As you draw closer to the Lord, you will also see how to overcome addictions and go beyond them to the abundant life that Christ promises in John 10:10.

Let me introduce you to a few thoughts that will change your outlook on life, and your understanding of the love of God.

God has a plan for your life!!!

The Bible has a lot to say about God's plan for us. It's a good plan, one you should consider following.

> *Therefore, if anyone is in Christ, he is a new creation; old things have passed away; behold, all things have become new. II Corinthians 5:17*

In other words, God is able to make you a new man or woman in Jesus Christ, not an improved one, but a brand new one. You can experience real life; you can have a new outlook with real peace and hope. You can be clean, not just physically delivered from drugs, but spiritually, mentally and emotionally clean. This may sound impossible right now, but as you read the scripture passages this course is based upon you will see that it may actually underestimate the new work that God is able to do in your life.

The new life described in II Corinthians 5:17 is quite different from the one we once lived. The old life was dominated by sin and rebellion. Isaiah 53:6 describes the problem this way:

> *All we like sheep have gone astray; we have turned everyone to his own way ....*

In other words, we turned away from God and His plan. We were like sheep that left the fold and strayed into the wilderness. Many of us were lured by a false shepherd who promised relief from pain but led us into bondage. If you are one of these sheep then you need to come home to the Good Shepherd – Jesus Christ.

God will enable you to resist the temptation to fall back into sin.

> *No temptation has overtaken you except such as is common to man; but God is faithful, who will not allow you to be tempted beyond what you are able, but with the temptation will also make the way of escape, that you may be able to bear it. I Corinthians 10:13*

This verse says that one of the keys to getting beyond addiction is to allow the Lord to meet you at the point of your weakness and deliver you rather than giving in to temptation and continuing to be bound up in sin. You may have been aware of this but still failed in your attempts to resist temptation. That is because you do not have the power within yourself to resist. Thank God that He enables you to resist temptation through the power of the Holy Spirit who dwells in every Christian. So sin no longer has to rule over you!

You have been created by Jesus Christ, and He has something special for you to do.

> *We are His workmanship, created in Christ Jesus for good works, which God prepared beforehand that we should walk in them. Ephesians 2:10*

You are not the product of shoddy workmanship. You have been created in Christ Jesus for good work that He has already prepared for you to do. God has a plan and He wants you to be involved in it. God has gifted you for a particular purpose and plan. When we went astray and turned to our own way, we were not following His plan and became frustrated and bitter. Return to God's plan. This is where you will find real meaning and purpose in life.

God has something special for each one of us to do. First of all, He has called us to worship Him and to enjoy His presence. He also has good work for each of us. The closer we are to Him, the more we understand His call or His distinct purpose for our lives.

God is thinking about you.

> *For I know the thoughts that I think toward you, says the LORD, thoughts of peace and not of evil, to give you a future and a hope. Jeremiah 29:11*

God gives you hope for your future. In fact, He is the hope for your future. You may have thought that things looked pretty hopeless. You may think that God has forgotten all about you. His Word tells us again that He still has a plan for your life; He hasn't forgotten you.

The King James Version says that God wants to give you "an expected end." That means that God wants to give you a conclusion that you can count on. Wouldn't you like to know that there is a finish you can trust? He has one. Wouldn't it be great to know that there is something solid and reliable that you can depend upon? There is.

Prepare to have some of your old ways of thinking challenged.

As we look directly into God's Word you will find that its message is radically different from what the world teaches. For example, the Bible teaches that:

- All of your sins can be completely forgiven (John 3:16-17, I John 1:7-9)
- Forgiveness, not vengeance is the way to be set free from the past (Romans 12:19, Ephesians 4:32, Hebrews 10:20)
- Christ-esteem is greater than self-esteem (Philippians 2:1-8)
- Being changed from the inside-out is better than allowing the habits of a sinful world to shape your thinking and behavior (Romans 12:1-2)
- We can find ourselves and the true meaning of life only by losing ourselves in Christ (Matthew 10:39)

Foundational Verses

There are sixteen Foundational Scripture passages in Appendix A. These verses are woven throughout each chapter. Begin reading them now and ask the Lord to show you how they apply to you.

Here are four verses to think about as we get started.

You are a new creation!

Therefore, if anyone is in Christ, he is a new creation; old things have passed away; behold, all things have become new. II Corinthians 5:17

God is thinking about you!

For I know the thoughts that I think toward you, says the LORD, thoughts of peace and not of evil, to give you a future and a hope. Jeremiah 29:11

In giving us Himself, God has given us all that we need.

According as His divine power has given to us all things that pertain to life and godliness, through the knowledge of Him who called us by glory and virtue. II Peter 1:3

Keep the faith until the end.

And let us not grow weary while doing good, for in due season we shall reap if we do not lose heart. Galatians 6:9

Photo Courtesy Bob Batson ©2011

Let the "Son" rise in your heart, as you start a new chapter in your life. The first step is yours, the first day of a new life of freedom in Christ

Transforming the Way We Think

Chapter 2

You are not what you think you are. But what you think, you are.
Dr. Howard G. Hendricks, *Living By The Book*

It was late one afternoon, and I was listening to a prison chaplain engage a five-time felon in conversation. "What are you going to do to keep from coming back to prison the sixth time?" He responded, "Well, I'm going to change the place I live, and I'm not going to hang out with the same guys anymore." The chaplain began to bear down on him. "You've tried that before and it didn't work." The guy began to get a little hot and defended his past mistakes as a drug addict and small-time dealer. After a while, the chaplain asked him if he had ever considered giving his life to Jesus. At that point, the inmate said, "Now I'm not ready for that. I think I can handle this problem without having to get religious about it. If I find out I'm wrong, I'll consider Jesus."

Here was a guy who needed to re-think this proposition. He needed much more than a few new friends or a new neighborhood. He desperately needed to redirect his thought life, particularly about Jesus.

Maybe you thought that all you needed was a little change in order to overcome your addiction. You may have attacked it on one front, usually in a physical way, "I can quit drinking if I stop going by the bar on the way home." Or you moved to another town to separate yourself from the people who got you in trouble. The battle against addiction is deeper than that. It is spiritual, physical, mental and emotional. It is waged first and most often in our thought life.

Maybe you have gone through countless numbers of rehab programs to get cleaned up; or you have been in prison and as a result you were physically separated from the addictive substance, only to find that when you were exposed to it again you returned to the pit of addiction. Why?

Your body may have undergone detox, but there were still poisonous thoughts running around in your mind. I often hear discussions on the prison yard that revolve around "drinkin' and druggin.'" The men in the conversations may claim that they don't want to return to that lifestyle, but listening to the discussions it is easy to tell where their hearts lie. Guess what happens when they are released from prison and are free to make their own choices? They drift back into the same lousy lifestyle that they were in before, and eventually they are back on the prison yard revisiting those same old conversations, only this time they have a longer prison sentence. It is a life-killing, vicious cycle.

What about rehabilitation? Isn't that the solution? *Rehabilitation* can accomplish a little, but most rehab programs avoid the core need in our lives. The Bible teaches us that we need to be *transformed*, not *re-formed* or *rehabilitated*. This is true for non-Christians and for Christians. We need to change our ways of thinking at the deepest level. We need to re-think our need for Jesus Christ and we need to agree with Him that our thought-life needs rebuilding.

As followers of Jesus Christ, we can have our thought-life rebuilt as the Holy Spirit works in us. This kind of radical change is necessary for everyone regardless of whether you struggle with drugs, alcohol, pornography, sexual addictions or other issues. The following scripture passage tells us how this important process takes place.

> *I beseech you therefore, brethren, by the mercies of God, that you present your bodies a living sacrifice, holy, acceptable to God, which is your reasonable service. And do not be conformed to this world, but be transformed (metamorphosed) by the renewing (renovation) of your mind, that you may prove what is that good and acceptable and perfect will of God. Romans 12:1-2*

Transformation requires a personal commitment over a long period of time. It is a call to submit your whole life to Christ. Thank God that you are not left alone in the process. The Holy Spirit is with you every step of the way.

Transformation also requires obedience on your part. God leads. He designs the plan. He works in you to strengthen your will, but you have to follow Him. This is a life-changing process that will reward you far more than anything else you have ever tried.

Let's take a deeper look into what the Apostle Paul is saying. "I beg you brother." This is very personal. Write your own name in the first sentence in place of "brethren" so that it reads, "I beg you therefore (<u>Your Name</u>) by the mercies of God to present your body as a living sacrifice, holy, acceptable unto God." Paul is crying out for you to give your life, your very physical life, to God. This is complete surrender to the will of God. This isn't a little change. It requires more than changing your habits or moving to another apartment. It is allowing God to direct the life that He has given you, and submitting to the authority of Christ through the Holy Spirit.

Let's face it; you really don't have much to lose. Your plans and mine didn't turn out very well. Following our desires led us to sorrow.

You might say, "But I have tried to live as a Christian." Many of us prayed the sinner's prayer. We knew we needed to change, but at that time we were not willing to submit our lives to Christ. Our cry may have been, "Lord please change my circumstances," but we were not willing to let Him change our lives. Give God the right to change your life. He loves you. You can trust Him with your life, so allow Him to change you as you submit your life to Him.

Holiness leads to happiness.

According to Romans 12:1-2, God's perfect plan is for us to live "holy" lives. Being "holy" simply means to live your life with the understanding that it is set apart for God.

There is a surprising benefit to living a holy life. The Bible teaches us that this is the way to true happiness and true fulfillment. Matthew 5:6 says *blessed are those who hunger and thirst after righteousness for they shall be filled.* To be blessed means that you are truly happy. Read Matthew 5:6 with that in mind. *Truly happy are those who hunger and thirst after righteousness for they shall be filled.* The ones who hunger and thirst after righteousness are truly happy.

So, the way to true happiness is to hunger and thirst, or to strongly desire, righteousness. That's a strange twist. I used to think that true happiness was found in going for the gusto, downing some brewskis, chasing girls, grabbing the big bucks. Nope. The Bible says that true happiness is found in seeking true righteousness or true holiness. Jesus says that those who strongly desire righteousness will be filled with happiness.

If you have been seeking real happiness by going for the gusto, then you are going in the wrong direction. It's like jumping in your car in North Carolina and driving east to get to California. You won't get there. It doesn't matter how many people have assured you that this is the right way. You won't get there. You need to pull out the one true road map, the spiritual GPS, and follow it. The Bible is the map.

The person Paul describes in Romans 12:1 is someone who is honestly hungering and thirsting after righteousness; this is a person who is heading in the right direction.

How can we change direction?

According to Romans 12:1-2, there are two keys to changing direction: 1) do not allow the world around you to shape your thinking, and 2) be transformed by the renewing of your mind.

First of all, stop allowing the pattern of the world around you to shape the way you think and act. Television, movies and other forms of mass media flood your mind with images of what a lost world calls success. It's glitzy, shiny and seems carefree. It says, "Have another drink." "If it feels good, do it." "You're 500 miles from home, forget about your wife."

Advertising can be very deceiving. It shows you the good time you can have downing a few beers, but it doesn't show you the drunk driving accident that may occur a few hours later, or the phone call from the girl who tells you that she is pregnant or has AIDS. One step in that direction leads to more until it becomes a pattern of life. Many people have been conformed to this pattern and later found themselves sitting in a jail cell wondering, "How did this happen? Where did I go wrong?"

These worldly images do not reveal the consequences of drinking that brewski, toking on that joint or getting that girl to sleep with you. However, we see the consequences of succumbing to these temptations all around us ... broken marriages, children growing up without their parents, violence, anger, depression, AIDS, other sexually transmitted diseases, poverty, and prison. It doesn't take a genius to see that the acts of *momentary pleasure* offered by the world pay off in *long-term suffering and pain*. This is the result of being conformed to the ways of an unbelieving world.

Where are you right now? If you are still investing your time watching graphic violence or sexual scenes on TV, reading junk novels or looking at pornography, then you are still being molded by the pattern of this world. These images create thoughts that eventually lead to actions.

You know that drinking poison will eventually damage your body or even kill you. Filling your mind with poisonous thoughts will do the same thing. Don't let it.

James 1:14-15 provides a clear picture of the problem caused when we are shaped by the pattern of this world.

> *But each one is tempted when he is drawn away by his own desires and enticed. Then, when desire has conceived, it gives birth to sin; and sin, when it is full-grown, brings forth death. James 1:14-15*

Each one of us has desires or needs; many of them are God-given. The problems are caused when we accept sinful, worldly means to fulfill our desires. Satan tempts us with attractive inducements in order to draw us into his web. He entices us into unhealthy relationships where we think we will find acceptance; he passes pornographic images across our eyes that offer some physical satisfaction. These solutions seem to offer some short-term fulfillment, but they lead to death and destruction.

James encourages us in verse 16, "Do not be deceived, my beloved brethren." Don't be fooled by the enemy's offer. Sexual pleasure outside of marriage will not bring long-term happiness or fulfillment. A hit of cocaine will not relieve the pain of abuse for more than a few hours, and it will leave you with a gnawing emptiness that is much worse. Do not be conformed to the pattern of this world.

Where are you spending your time? What kind of pictures do you have posted inside your locker, stuck in a drawer or hidden in a folder on your computer? The influencers in this sinful world want you to open your ears, your eyes and your mouth so they can pour their poisonous mixture into your life. Don't let them.

Secondly, take the path that God provides to escape the pit of addiction. God calls us to be transformed by the renewal of our minds. "Transformed" literally means to undergo metamorphosis. Metamorphosis is the process that transforms a caterpillar into a butterfly. That's an interesting comparison. Do you ever feel like you are crawling through life like a caterpillar? God wants to give you a new life so you can float through it like a butterfly. You may have noticed that butterflies enjoy a much better life than caterpillars, and they have a much better view of the world too. No one tries to burn their house down either. Wouldn't you like to move out of the weeds and into the trees? You can. Submit your life to God's process of transformation.

How does this change take place? According to Romans 12:2, it is caused by the renewal of our minds. To renew literally means "to renovate." If you have ever renovated a house, you know this isn't a minor change; it is a major overhaul.

You may have thought that your personal life just needed a little touch-up in order to fix the problems. You know, just a coat of paint here or there, and hammer in a few loose nails. Not so. Imagine living in a home with a leaky roof for ten years. The ceiling gets wet and starts to rot, the foundation sags, the plumbing begins to fail and the drywall begins to grow mold after years of neglect. Does this house need a little touch-up or a complete renovation? It needs a complete renovation.

Your personal life needs renovation too. You are not alone; all of us suffered from a lack of spiritual attention through most of our lives. We have been rotting away because we have taken on the same pattern of thinking and actions of an unbelieving world. On the inside, we are a lot like the rest of the houses in the neighborhood. In other words, we have been conformed to this world. In order to be truly happy and fulfilled we must be renovated inside-out. God wants to make you into a beautiful home where the Holy Spirit dwells. That is a major project, but He can do it.

How can we renovate our thinking?

Renewing our minds is a process that is similar to renovating a house. It requires an investment of time and effort.

According to the Bible, we are renewed by reading God's Word, praying and worshipping the Lord. As we continue the process of renovation, our thought life is radically changed just as a house is radically changed by the removal of the rotten flooring, crumpling drywall, old appliances, wiring and plumbing. The old stuff is removed and the new is installed.

There are a lot of Bible passages that help to explain this process. We're going to look at a few of them in this chapter and you will see more as you continue reading.

This process of cleaning and renewing is also described another way in the book of Ephesians.

Just as Christ also loved the church and gave Himself for her, that He might sanctify and cleanse her with the washing of water by the word. Ephesians 5:25-26

In other words, our minds are cleansed by reading the Bible just as our bodies are washed clean in pure water. When you soak up God's Word, you are taking a spiritual shower that cleanses your heart and mind. You are refreshed. You have new energy. You may even smell better.

Does your work environment seem dirty? Not just with literal dirt, but with swearing and lying and noise and anger that many jobs or home situations are saturated in. Sometimes the sinfulness of your surroundings makes it seem like you are drowning in a sea of mud and muck. Even in these situations, I encourage you to draw aside with Jesus during a private time of day, open your Bible and allow the Holy Spirit to wash you in the water of God's Word. Maybe the only place you can go to get away from the noise is the bathroom. Go. Sit down with your Bible and pray for ten minutes. Your spirit and soul will be cleansed, and you will feel refreshed.

You may live in prison. Make your bunk a haven for Bible reading and prayer. Take a small Bible with you if you work on the road squad, and read it while going from the prison to the work site. God wants to meet you in the middle of your day, in the middle of your trials. He wants to transform you, and renew your mind by the power of the Holy Spirit.

Reading the Bible will bring you closer to Jesus.

This is the main reason for reading the Bible. According to II Peter 1:2-3, God has given us all things that pertain to life and godliness through the knowledge of Him (Jesus) who has called us by glory and virtue.

God has given us all things we need for life in the knowledge of Jesus Christ. This is a bold statement but it is true. All we need for life is found in Jesus. It isn't found in a bottle or a pill or a dirty movie, and it isn't found in owning more stuff or getting a promotion either. It is found in Jesus.

Jesus is our Savior, our hero, our role model. The more time we spend with Jesus, the more we become like Him.

> *But we all, with unveiled face, beholding as in a mirror the glory of the Lord, are being transformed into the same image from glory to glory, just as by the Spirit of the Lord.*
> *II Corinthians 3:18*

Isn't this a wonderful picture? As we look into the face of Jesus, we become more like Him; and the more like Jesus we become, the less we care about the addictive thoughts and substances that once held us captive. You may remember when Moses spent time with God on Mt. Sinai that he came down to the Israelite's camp with his face glowing. Our faces glow too as we spend time with Jesus.

The Bible is the most powerful book ever written. God uses it to reveal our innermost thoughts and motives. If you want to understand yourself, read the Bible.

> *For the word of God is living and powerful, and sharper than any two-edged sword, piercing even to the division of soul and spirit, and of joints and marrow, and is a discerner of the thoughts and intents of the heart.*
> *Hebrews 4:12*

God's Word addresses the issues of life. It deals with spiritual and mental issues, physical issues and it discerns our true motives (the thoughts and intents of the heart). This isn't a dead book; it is the living Word of God.

Studying the Bible is also very practical.

> *All Scripture is given by inspiration of God, and is profitable for doctrine, for reproof, for correction, for instruction in righteousness, that the man of God may be*

complete, thoroughly equipped for every good work.
II Timothy 3:16-17

God teaches you as you read the Bible. His instruction stops you when you veer in the wrong direction; it puts you back on the right path, and it keeps you there. The result of your study of God's Word is that you, as a man or woman of God, will be thoroughly prepared for all good works.

So, the Bible contains the counsel needed to renew your mind and God promises that by reading and studying it, you will be prepared for ALL good works. Is kicking addictive behavior a good work? You bet!

The Holy Spirit helps us to understand the Bible.
Maybe you have read some of the Bible before and it didn't seem to be quite as powerful as these verses describe it to be. I have some good news. Jesus Christ sent someone to bring it to life for you. Before He went to the cross, Jesus promised to send another counselor or helper just like Him to guide you into truth. Your helper is the Holy Spirit.

> *And I will pray the Father, and He will give you another Helper, that He may abide with you forever, the Spirit of truth, whom the world cannot receive, because it neither sees Him nor knows Him; but you know Him, for He dwells with you and will be in you.* *John 14:16-17*

> *But the Helper, the Holy Spirit, whom the Father will send in My name, He will teach you all things, and bring to your remembrance all things that I said to you.* *John 14:26*

Jesus did not save you and leave you here to do the best you can. He never intended for you to fight the battle against sin on your own. He sent the Holy Spirit to counsel and comfort you. According to John 14:16-17, the Holy Spirit dwells in you if you are a believer in Jesus Christ. The passage in John 14:26 says that the Holy Spirit helps you understand the Bible. He brings it to life. As you seek counsel in God's Word and ask the Holy Spirit to help you, He will teach you all things and bring to mind the scripture passages that enable you to make good decisions. In the process, your thought-life is radically changed.

Nothing is more powerful than God's Word when you are seeking His will to make decisions, to find the proper instruction for righteousness, to equip you for all good works, or to understand the motives and thoughts in your heart. Sixty minutes of prayer and reading His Word is worth much more than the advice of worldly counselors who do not have the mind of Christ. So, if you want to change the way you think, ask the Lord to give you understanding in His Word, then open it and read.

God also gives us Godly people to help transform us.

As the Lord directs us, we are able to counsel one another. I have benefited many times from the counsel of people who know the Lord and are students of the Bible.

> *Now I myself am confident concerning you, my brethren, that you also are full of goodness, filled with all knowledge, able also to admonish one another. Romans 15:14*

God uses our experiences with Him to transform each other too.

The trials in your life are not wasted. In fact, as you and I walk with the Lord, He uses our experiences to encourage those who are enduring the same trials. Because of your experiences, you are able to see problems through the eyes of others who are currently going through them. You are able to relate, you empathize with them, and you can extend the grace that God has given you to others who need it too.

> *Blessed be the God and Father of our Lord Jesus Christ, the Father of mercies and God of all comfort, who comforts us in all our tribulation that we may be able to comfort those who are in any trouble, with the comfort with which we ourselves are comforted by God. II Corinthians 1:3-4*

You can encourage, comfort and strengthen others with the comfort you have received from God. As you encourage or disciple people who are struggling with addiction, be sure that you continually direct them to Jesus Christ. He is the God of all comfort. Pray with them and pray for them. Lead them to the Bible for answers.

Conclusion

God can change you. He can set you free from bondage to addiction so you can enjoy a life with real happiness and meaning.

Jesus Christ will transform your life. He wants to give you His peace, His purpose and His joy. Isn't this better than the life that you have been living?

Jesus opened the door for you and me to have new life when He shed His blood for your and my sins. Because of the blood of Jesus, you can be forgiven; you can have real life now, and you can spend eternity with Him in heaven. Thank God that He didn't stop there. He sent the Holy Spirit to counsel, comfort and to change the way you think. This is vital as you throw addictions out the back door with the trash and begin enjoying the clean, new, abundant life that Jesus Christ has to offer. God who has power over death and life also has power over the sins that would set you back.

If you are a Christian, you should begin the process of change by applying Romans 12:1-2. Do not be conformed to this world. Ask the Lord to show you how to avoid being molded into the shape that it wants you to take. Ask yourself how you are affected by the movies and programs you watch on television, by the magazines and books you read, or the Internet sites you visit. Ask the Lord to convict you of sin in the areas that are harmful to you. Then follow the Apostle Paul's plea not to be conformed to the pattern of this world.

Be transformed by the renewal of your mind. By reading through this chapter, you have already begun the process of transforming your life. Continue to focus on the things of the Lord (Colossians 3:1-2). Pray, meditate upon His Word and ask the Lord to show you how to apply the scripture verses in this chapter. Please, please, please pick up your Bible; read 2-4 chapters every day and ask the Holy Spirit to give you understanding.

PART II

BIBLICAL VIEWS OF ADDICTION

How Did We Descend into Addiction?
Addiction as Idolatry
Other Biblical Views of Addiction

"How did I ever get here?"

You may have asked this question when you wound up sitting in a holding cell.

With approximately 27 million Americans either using illicit drugs regularly or being "heavy drinkers,"[2] a question that many people have asked themselves is "How did I descend into such a lousy way of living?" In chapter 3 we will see what the Bible says about this path to addiction. Then you will know how to avoid it so that you never pass this way again.

---

[2] U.S. Substance Abuse and Mental Health Services Administration.

How did we descend into addiction?

Chapter 3

Victory in the Christian life is not me overcoming sin.
Victory is Christ overcoming me.
Wayne Barber, pastor and author

Have you ever asked a child what they wanted to be when they grew up? Some may say a teacher. Others want to be a doctor or nurse, a store owner, a computer technician or a musician. A lot of kids may tell you that they plan to play in the NBA. No child will say that they want to be a drug addict or an old drunk.

How does someone move from a life of dreams to a life of addiction? This is a lousy way to live and God has a better plan. Having lived in addiction, how can you move from this misery to a life of freedom and hope?

We're going to look for the answers to these questions, but before we do, it would be helpful to define the problem just to make sure that you and I are talking about the same thing.

Dr. Edward Welch, Director of Biblical Counseling with the Christian Counseling Education Foundation, authored an excellent book on addiction entitled *Addictions: A Banquet in the Grave*. In it, he defines addiction as:

> *Bondage to the rule of a substance, activity, or state of mind, which then becomes the center of life, defending itself from the truth so that even bad consequences don't bring repentance, and leading to further estrangement from God.*[3]

Let's break this down. According to Dr. Welch, addiction has five characteristics.

1) First of all, addiction is bondage. Addicts are enslaved to one or a combination of three things: substances – alcohol, mariju-

---

[3] Edward T. Welch, *Addictions: A Banquet in the Grave* (Phillipsburg: P&R Publishing Company, 2001).

ana, cocaine, tobacco, etc. activities – gambling, watching pornographic movies, looking at pornographic pictures, reading porn novels, having sex with someone you are not married to, etc.-- a state of mind – thoughts about these substances or activities, feelings of power over someone, feelings of acceptance by someone, etc.

2)   These addictive substances, activities or thoughts become the center of your life. They occupy your first thoughts in the morning. They consume your money. They are the source of some pleasure. Your life begins to revolve around them.

3)   Then we became so deceived in our addiction that we defended our actions against the truth. You may have said, "I'm not addicted, I can quit anytime I want!" "Nobody has actually seen me snorting coke so no one really knows that I'm doing it." "What's the big deal? Everybody has a drink or two after work." "Sex with different women is normal. They do it on TV all the time."

4)   Even bad consequences don't bring us to a point of repentance. Losing your job, having your wife leave you or getting arrested doesn't motivate you to change your ways. You may have felt sorry for your actions, but you lacked the inner conviction and will power to change.

5)   The result is that you fall further and further away from God. You may have given up on your relationship with Jesus. Satan draws you further into his trap and attempts to close the door behind you. Thank Jesus for not giving up on you.

So, addiction made us a slave to something that dominated our lives, deceived us and separated us from God. Look at this for a moment. Addiction is not only wrong, it isn't even smart!

What motivated us to descend to such a place?

The reasons for starting a bad habit are usually different than the reasons for continuing it. You may have smoked the first marijuana joint because "everybody else was doing it" and you felt pressured into it. You may have broken into a house or committed some other crime just to see what it was like to engage in forbidden behavior. You continued because the thing you were doing gave you some momentary thrill. Many former addicts made the mistake of starting an addictive habit in order to meet a real need.

They used drugs or alcohol to escape rejection from someone they loved. They drank in order to blur the images of abuse as a child. Many war veterans defeated the enemy in the field but fell victim to drugs and alcohol once they came home. They drank, shot up, smoked or took a pill in order to forget the past for a while.

Maybe you fell under the spell of someone in order to fulfill your sense of self-worth only to find that they were more interested in using you than in helping you.

Your addiction may have offered a brief opportunity to forget past painful experiences, to cure your shyness, to avoid pain, to fit in with others or to reduce your sense of loneliness. The addiction seemed to provide some sort of power or freedom.

Maybe you believed the lie that a bottle of booze, a joint or a little walk on the wild side would add something good to your life.

You may have allowed the devil to isolate you, and to convince you that you were the only one who had ever been dealt such a serious problem of rejection or abuse. So you drank, you shot up or you smoked to cope with the pain.

In any case, once you were hooked, the benefit faded and you continued to engage in the addictive activity to alleviate the pain or emptiness of not doing it. Now you realize that the painful cost for giving in to temptation was much greater than the temporary benefits received from doing it.

Giving into temptation is always a bad idea. The Bible warns us not to be enticed and deceived by this kind of thinking. The following account in Proverbs 9 shows us what happens when we are not prepared to deal with temptation. This example is clearly about sexual addiction, but it applies to other addictions as well.

> *A foolish woman is clamorous; she is simple, and knows nothing. For she sits at the door of her house, On a seat by the highest places of the city, to call to those who pass by, Who go straight on their way: "Whoever is simple, let him turn in here"; And as for him who lacks understanding, she says to him, "Stolen water is sweet, And bread eaten in secret is pleasant." But he does not know that the dead are there, that her guests are in the depths of hell.*
> *Proverbs 9:13-18*

We can learn a few lessons from this young man in Proverbs 9. This scripture provides a frighteningly accurate picture of how we were enticed. Like this young man, we harbored lust in our hearts and the enemy knew how to entice us. We started by just wandering by the door of the crack house, or experimenting with a little marijuana, or looking at soft pornographic magazines like most sports or bodybuilding publications. Maybe you stopped by someone's house just to say "Hi" knowing that her husband wasn't home.

The thing that you were going after to get a little thrill may have been illegal, or maybe you knew that your parents wouldn't approve. Whatever the case, you bought the same line as the young man in Proverbs 9 that stolen waters are sweet and things done in secret are pleasant. As a result, you began to slide down the slippery slope from temptation into bondage.

James 1:14 describes the problem this way:

But every man is tempted, when he is drawn away of his own desires (or lust) and is enticed.

When a person is carried away by their own lust, then they are ripe for the picking. This is probably what happened to you. At first, you didn't realize that you were descending into an addiction. You may have believed, "I found my thrill on Blueberry Hill." Thinking that you were flying high, you were really descending into the pit of addiction. Later when your eyes opened, you were horrified to see that it was filled with dead men's bones. The thing that you used for your pleasure began to use you. Eventually, you were bound to it.

How did you get hooked into such a miserable condition? Like me and millions of others, you were baited and enticed by a crafty fisherman – the devil.

A good fisherman knows how to attract fish. He baits them with something that they want, like worms, minnows or some type of lure. Satan uses the same tactics. He baits the hook with something you really like. He won't meet you at the bar with an unattractive woman or a drink that tastes like stale water. He dances someone out who looks good, and he fills your cup with something that tastes good. What you did not see or care about at the time is that he was baiting you. Just like the poor fish that saw something really good on the line, you did not realize that you were caught until the hook was set and he was reeling you into his boat.

Do we have to wind up on Satan's line?

As fallen men, we are bent toward temptation and sin, so we naturally lean toward addiction to one thing or another. In the flesh, we naturally look for some type of physical or emotional satisfaction. The lust to satisfy these thirsts provides Satan with an opportunity to bait and catch us.

This situation can be changed by a relationship with Jesus Christ. When you are born again of the Spirit, you are given new spiritual life. That is what Jesus told Nicodemus in the third chapter of the Book of John. Nicodemus was a highly educated Pharisee, one of the seventy men who ruled the people of Israel. He came to Jesus to find how to enter the kingdom of God. Jesus said, "Nic, you must be born again." In other words, every man has to start life as a spiritual baby. When you are born again, you have new spiritual life. As a result, the spirit can control your body and mind. Until then, you allowed your physical and emotional desires to control you. Those desires were very deceiving and they exposed you to Satan's temptations; however, as a new Christian you grow in your relationship with Jesus, and the desire for Satan's temptations fade away. This wasn't possible before you were born again.

In the fourth chapter of the book of John, Jesus met a woman at Jacob's well outside of the city of Samaria. This woman had spent her life seeking fulfillment through short-term physical relationships. Attempting to meet a real need through unrighteous means, she fell victim to the temptations of the enemy time and time again. She had been married five times and was now living with a man she wasn't married to. Clearly she had been searching for someone or something to satisfy her thirst for love and acceptance. This is a tragedy common to young women who want someone to care for them. Desperate for love, they fall victim to men who aren't interested in love but are looking for someone to satisfy their own lust. Once a young woman has been used this way, it can become a pattern of life, and they continue to seek short-term physical relationships as a substitute for real love.

Jesus understood this woman's real need, and He loved her right where she was. Sitting at Jacob's well, He used it as an illustration to diagnose her problem – she had been drinking from the wrong well. All of the solutions she had tried were doomed to fail because they did not fulfill her deepest need. Jesus responded with real love, grace and truth. He said, "If you knew the gift of God and who it is that says to you, 'Give me to drink', you would have asked of him and he would have given you living water." He told her, "Whoever drinks of this water (from Jacob's well) will thirst again but whoever drinks of the water that I shall give him shall never thirst but the water that I shall give him shall be in him a well of water springing up into everlasting life!"

Jesus pointed her, and He points us, to Himself as the only source to satisfy the deepest needs of life. The addiction problems that you have experienced can be summed up by saying, "You have been drinking from the wrong wells." You have been looking for love in all the wrong places. You bought the lie that drugs would give you real peace, that drinking with the guys would make you feel accepted. You cannot find true peace, true joy and fulfillment from wells that provide temporary relief, no matter how much you drink. Real joy, real peace and real fulfillment are found in drinking the living water given only through a relationship with Jesus Christ.

So here is the good news. If you are a believer in Jesus Christ, then you can drink every day from the well that springs up into everlasting life. There is no need to consume the poisonous water that we used to draw from those wells of the past.

How can we avoid this trap in the future?

You followed the same downward spiral that many others have followed for centuries. I want you to recognize it so you will know how to avoid it.

Dr. Welch describes the descent into addiction as a path that begins with unpreparedness and moves to friendship with the addictive thoughts or substance. Then an addict becomes infatuated with what is controlling him and actually begins to love it. The path leads further to betrayal and finally to worshipping what binds you. Another way to look at this downward path is to see it move from acts of sin to slavery to tragedy.[4]

---

[4] Edward T. Welch, *Addictions: A Banquet in the Grave* (Phillipsburg: P&R Publishing Company, 2001), 66.

26

This has been the course of man's fall since creation. Our great, great, great … Grandfather Adam fell into sin and we are made of the same stuff. Just as Adam and Eve were curious about the location of the tree of the knowledge of good and evil, their descendents are also curious about forbidden fruit. Our disobedient nature and denial of the consequences of sin led us to try it. We became infatuated with the forbidden fruit and increased our involvement with it over time. At some point, the hook was set and we were in trouble. Like the drunkard in Proverbs 23:35, we experienced some dreadful misery, but we kept seeking the very thing that had caused the problem.

They have struck me, but I was not hurt. They have beaten me, but I did not feel it. When shall I awake, that I may seek another drink? Proverbs 23:35

This unfortunate picture looks all too familiar. Reeling from drunkenness that has destroyed his life, this fellow has been beaten without feeling it and passes out. When he wakes up, he will look for another drink. Sin practiced over time leads to slavery and tragedy.

Here is some good news. Even though the initial sin in disobeying God's warnings led to slavery and tragedy, it does not have to remain that way. God's grace has rescued countless men like you and me. In his love He seeks us, and by His blood He forgives us and cleanses us from all sin. Thank God that as new creations in Christ, He gives us a new spiritual nature that leads us toward the Lord and away from the pit of addiction. So God can set you free from bondage, and He can keep you free from ever falling back again.

What should you do right now? If you want to avoid sliding back into the pit, then grab hold of Jesus' hand and let Him pull you out. If you are living in a sinful situation, flee. If you are tempted to go by the crack house or to use some other abusive form of relief, don't. When the enemy tempts you to take one of these destructive options, pick up your Bible, read it and let the Lord transform you by renewing your mind. If you have not been in fellowship with Christians, find a good, local church and go there this week. Get into an environment where you are surrounded by healthy Christians.

As a warning for the future, we are going to look back at one Biblical picture of the trap and tragedy of addiction. God's Word faithfully portrays the sinfulness and silliness of man so that we can see the danger and avoid it. The story that we are going to look at for a moment takes place during the period of Judges in 1200 B.C. It is about a man named Samson who was extraordinarily gifted, but he failed miserably in his attempts to deal with temptation. His life was marked with signs that God uses to warn us from taking the same path of destruction.

Samson was one of the most gifted judges who ever governed Israel. He was called by God before birth to be a Nazarite, a special servant of God. He was strong and evidently good-looking. He had leadership abilities; however, he was also one of the poorest judges in the history of the nation until the closing moments of his life. What was his problem? The gifts given him for the glory of God and service to Israel were used for his own selfish pleasure. He was a very selfish public official who permitted his physical desires to rule his life, and he used his tremendous gifts and power to fulfill those desires. It wasn't supposed to be that way.

Samson was a Nazarite, a man who was supposed to be wholly consecrated to God. In Numbers 6:1-21, Moses proscribes the three aspects of the Nazarite vow. As an outward expression of an inward separation unto God, a Nazarite would not: 1) eat anything made of grapes, 2) touch a dead carcass whether animal or human, or 3) cut his hair until his vow was fulfilled. Over time, Samson broke all three of these vows as he descended lower into the pit of addiction.

Let's look at a few snapshots of Samson's life.

> *Now Samson went down to Timnah, and saw a woman in Timnah of the daughters of the Philistines. So he went up and told his father and mother, saying, "I have seen a woman in Timnah of the daughters of the Philistines; now therefore, get her for me as a wife." Then his father and mother said to him, "Is there no woman among the daughters of your brethren, or among all my people, that you must go and get a wife from the uncircumcised Philistines?" And Samson said to his father, "Get her for me, for she pleases me well." Judges 14:1-3*

In Judges 14:1-3, the first report we have of young Samson is that he is heading down the road to Timnah. This Philistine town was in a prime wine-grape region. As a Nazarite, he wasn't supposed to go near it. Samson is already off on the wrong road.

What led Samson down the road to Timnah? I don't know. Maybe he was curious about this forbidden village or about the Philistine girls who lived there. Led by his physical desires, Samson put himself in a risky position and was not prepared to deal with temptation. He went down to Timnah and saw a woman. As a Hebrew, he was not supposed to marry a woman of another faith. Why was he enticed by this Philistine woman? Maybe he was tempted simply because he wasn't supposed to be there or have contact with Philistine girls. Remember the lie in Proverbs 9, "stolen waters are sweet." Whatever he was thinking, Samson was harboring lust in his heart, and Satan knew how to draw it out.

> So Samson went down to Timnah with his father and mother, and came to the vineyards of Timnah. Now to his surprise, a young lion came roaring against him. And the Spirit of the LORD came mightily upon him, and he tore the lion apart as one would have torn apart a young goat, though he had nothing in his hand. But he did not tell his father or his mother what he had done. Then he went down and talked with the woman; and she pleased Samson well. Judges 14:5-7

God permitted the enemy to roar against Samson in order to warn him from taking this destructive path. Apart from the mercy of God, the lion would have killed him. In His wonderful grace, God was warning Samson, and protecting him at the same time.

Perhaps you remember a time in the past when God spared you from the full consequence of your sin. Maybe you were saved from being in a fight in which someone was badly hurt or killed. Your first reaction was probably, "Thank God that I wasn't there. I'll never do that again!" Maybe you were crawling out of the back window of someone's house as her husband was walking through the front door. "Thank God that I was saved from that. I'll never do that again!" Over time, the scare of the lion became just a distant memory and you went back to the house. The barrier that God put up to keep you from falling into temptation became just a little speed bump on your way to the next thrill. The same thing happened to Samson.

Notice what he did later when he came down the same road.

> *After some time, when he returned to get her, he turned aside to see the carcass of the lion. And behold, a swarm of bees and honey were in the carcass of the lion. He took some of it in his hands and went along, eating. When he came to his father and mother, he gave some to them, and they also ate. But he did not tell them that he had taken the honey out of the carcass of the lion. Judges 14:8-9*

He wandered over toward the dead carcass and lo and behold, there was something sweet in it. He even took some of the honey and gave it to his parents. Why didn't he tell them where it came from? As a Nazarite, he wasn't supposed to touch the lion's carcass. Having backslidden, Samson didn't sense any conviction to avoid it, but he didn't want his parents to know that he wasn't the good Nazarite boy that he used to be. He had already begun falling into compromise and losing his professed commitment to God. The devotion he had for the LORD was fading away as he was enticed by the Philistine woman and the sweetness in the dead carcass. His vow was no longer in his heart; it was just an outward show.

Many a young church-goer has experienced the same thing. Having heard the gospel preached in church or by your godly grandmother, you knew the truth, but the temptations of an intriguing world led you deeper into sin. You fell.

Now that you are interested once again in the things of the Lord, you may be tempted to go back to the old ways. There are some old carcasses from your past that are tempting you with the promise of a little sweetness. Satan, your enemy, is enticing you with thoughts of old relationships or of drinking, druggin', barhopping, chasing women or men. Remember that there isn't anything positive in those old addictive habits, no matter how sweet they may taste at first.

I have worked with hundreds of men in prison who are starting their new life with the Lord when suddenly they receive a letter from an old girlfriend. They began thinking, *Maybe I should call her just to check up on her. She wasn't such a bad girl. I remember the time when ... .* Wake up! Don't fall for this one. You don't need to call anyone you were living in sin with just to see how they are doing. Satan, your enemy, is just trying to entice you into looking for a little sweetness in that old relationship. Don't call. Don't go. Don't think about it.

Someone who has been delivered from drug addiction may be tempted to stop and see his old friends on the way home from work. *I just want to see the old gang for a few minutes, to let them see how well I'm doing.* There was a young man who returned to prison a few years ago. When I saw him on the yard, I asked him what he was doing back. He told me that he stopped by a friend's house on the way home from work one day. The guy offered him some coke, so he joined him. Within a month he had a $500 a day drug habit, and he stole some equipment from his employer in order to finance his addiction. Now he's back in prison.

Take note of this. When the enemy tempts you to re-visit your old stomping grounds, don't even entertain the thought. Take yourself straight home and thank God that you are free from the mess that you were once enslaved to.

Maybe you think, *A glimpse at that magazine wouldn't hurt. It's not even considered porn anymore. Besides, it's nothing like the stuff I used to look at on the Internet.* Make no mistake, compromise kills. Stay away from the things that can draw you back into a lifestyle of sin and slavery.

Remember, according to II Corinthians 5:17 you are a new creation in Christ Jesus, *old things have passed away* and all things have become new. There isn't anything in those old carcasses that belong in your new life.

In Samson's case, you can see a habit of compromise in the life of this very gifted man. He was doing nothing to cultivate his relationship with God, but he was doing all he could to cultivate his taste for sin and rebellion. This formerly good Nazarite boy was chasing wine and women; by sowing to the flesh, he would eventually reap the fruit of it. Be warned. Friendship with sin looks appealing on the front end, but it leads to a life of slavery and tragedy.

By the time we reach the sixteenth chapter in Judges, Samson's marriage has failed, and he has experienced a number of other problems, all of which God delivered him from. In His grace, God did not forsake Samson. In His grace, God has not forsaken you either. But Samson's sinful desires were beginning to take control of his life.

Now Samson went to Gaza and saw a harlot there, and went in to her. Judges 16:1

Notice that Samson is no longer concerned that he should first marry a girl before he has sex with her. By the time you reach Judges 16:1, he is only interested in fulfilling his physical desires, regardless of what God has said about it.

In addition, Gaza was a stronghold of the Philistines, and Samson was not supposed to be near there. He was guilty of having sex with someone he wasn't married to, and he was also consorting with a woman of another faith even though he knew better. The men of Israel had been enticed by the Moabite women in the wilderness generations earlier, and it led to idolatry and God's judgment (Numbers 24). Samson is courting danger. God is long-suffering, but His judgment eventually falls when you continue in willful sin.

The further Samson goes, the more he wanders away from God and toward the enemy's trap. Samson seems convinced that he can get out of any trouble that he finds himself in. Blinded by pride, Samson does not realize that God was the one who had delivered him out of trouble time and time again. He feels comfortable with sin and confident that he can get himself out of any trap that the enemy lays for him.

You may have fallen victim to the same trap. In His mercy, God delivered you from punishment that you deserved, but you came to the conclusion that it was your own strength, intellect or luck that delivered you. This kind of thinking eventually cost Samson his freedom, his strength and his eyesight. Wouldn't it be good for you to stop before it costs you the same things?

Afterward it happened that he loved a woman in the Valley of Sorek, whose name was Delilah. Judges 16:4

Sorek was another grape growing region controlled by the Philistines. Samson wasn't supposed to be there, but having reduced his Nazarite vow to only an outward show, he didn't sense any inner conviction for his sin. He had broken God's commandment against adultery so often that his conscience was seared and it didn't bother him anymore. This gifted man had become totally deceived in his addiction.

Believing he was free to pursue any pleasure he wanted, Samson had become enslaved to his lust. Having won so many battles, he thought he was invincible. In reality, he was completely unaware of his real circumstances. Satan had cast the line and he is about to bring Samson in as a prize.

You may be familiar with the account of Samson & Delilah's brief interlude. This is a strange story. As you read through the sixteenth chapter in the book of Judges, you cannot help but notice how cavalier and perverted the man had become. In Judges 16:5-19, Samson was so lost in his relationship with Delilah that he was in bed with her, knowing that his enemies were waiting in the same room with them. He was playing games with the woman who wanted to betray him into the hands of the enemy. It even appears that Samson had fallen into sadomasochism; Delilah asked him three times "what must I do to afflict you." This once respected judge in Israel had descended to the level of a sexual deviant. Without realizing it, he had become enslaved by his desires. In the process, he betrayed his relationship with God and forgot his responsibility to the people of Israel.

This reads like a modern-day account of a respected public official who falls deep into sexual sin. It makes you wonder how someone with so much going for him could stoop so low. Well, he probably didn't get there overnight. The fall from God-fearing, wife-loving family man to sexual perversion usually happens step-by-step as Satan draws a man further and further into his net. Maybe he went browsing on a website that he didn't need to look at and wound up sliding down into a world of Internet pornography. This was the first step on the road to Timnah. Like Samson, sin would take him further than he ever intended to go and cost more than he ever wanted to pay.

Most addicts believe that they can manage their addiction. Samson was no different. Looking at his life from this end, it is easy to see how he descended from curiosity or friendship with addiction to infatuation to love for it and finally to betrayal of his responsibilities and worshipping his addiction. By the time he met Delilah, he was already enslaved.

Do a little heart inspection. Look at the warning signs and see if there is any compromise in your life right now. Have you in any way started down the road to Timnah? Are you playing around with pornography on the Internet? Do you have any dope stashed in an old coffee can? Do you find yourself reminiscing about the old days when you were living in the pit of addiction? If you are justifying your actions by saying that it is just "a little sin," then you are already at risk. Repent, turn around and go back home.

Samson finally experienced unexpected tragedy:

> *And she said, "The Philistines are upon you, Samson!" So he awoke from his sleep, and said, "I will go out as before, at other times, and shake myself free!" But he did not know that the LORD had departed from him. Then the Philistines took him and put out his eyes, and brought him down to Gaza. They bound him with bronze fetters, and he became a grinder in the prison. Judges 16:20-21*

Samson allowed Delilah to remove the last vestige of his Nazarite vow – his long hair. At that point, God departed Samson's life and left him to his own sin. Verse twenty says, "He did not know that the LORD had departed from him." That is one of the saddest verses in the Bible. Samson's relationship with God was so distant that he didn't realize that God had left him. It was as if God was a former friend with whom he had lost contact. He didn't know that God had left town. He was so blind in his addiction that he allowed the men of Philistia to take him and burn out his eyes with a hot sear.

What a sad point in Samson's life. This gifted man had never cultivated a relationship God. God had warned him over and over until he finally turned Samson over to his own passions and they destroyed him.

There are a lot of similarities in the life of Samson to our addictive experiences. Here are just a few:

- We permitted our feet to take us somewhere that we did not need to go.
- We allowed the lust of our eyes and our flesh to control our judgment.
- We tasted the addiction and kind of liked it.
- Having tried it, we lost conviction and increased the frequency of our sin.
- Suddenly we were trapped and were willing to give up our home, family, job, even our relationship with God in order to continue the relationship with our addiction.
- Like Samson, we were left blind and grinding in the prison house.

Are you at risk? Maybe you have been calling someone while you are at work so your wife won't find out, or you just bought a bag of pot to smoke while the kids are away this weekend, or you rented an X-rated movie to watch tonight, or the six pack is in the refrigerator and you are just waiting for it to get cold. If you are flirting with addiction, I urge you to read the signs in Samson's life and get off of the path to Timnah. The road to Calvary is the only way to go. The gate may be narrow and the way may be difficult, but this is the way which leads to life (Matthew 7:14).

I recently saw a church marquee that read, "The way to heaven – turn right and stay straight." That's good advice for someone on the wrong road who needs to turn to Jesus.

Now that we know how we descended into addiction, how do we get out?

Remarkably, God redeemed Samson. You may have thought that his willful disobedience doomed Samson to eternity in hell. How could anyone who failed so miserably and walked away from God so frequently ever be forgiven? Well, Samson was forgiven. In fact, he is mentioned in Hebrews 11:32 as one of the men of faith from the Old Testament!

Jesus can redeem you too. You may have lived a life of sin. You may think that you are the biggest hypocrite who ever lived and that God could never forgive you. He can and what's more, He wants to. II Peter 3:9 tells us that it is not God's will that any should perish, but that all should come to repentance. That is why He has been so patient with us. You can come to Him today. Just confess your sins, ask God to forgive you by the blood of Jesus Christ, and you will be saved forever. He will give you a new life here and now so that you can live free from addiction forever.

Where do we go from here?

> *Therefore we also, since we are surrounded by so great a cloud of witnesses, <u>let us lay aside every weight, and the sin which so easily ensnares us, and let us run with endurance the race that is set before us, looking unto Jesus, the author and finisher of our faith,</u> who for the joy that was set before Him endured the cross, despising the shame, and has sat down at the right hand of the throne of God. Hebrews 12:1-2*

Lay aside the sinful habits that have weighed you down. Run with patience the race set before you by keeping your eyes on Jesus Christ.

Your ascent out of addiction begins when you accept Jesus Christ as your LORD and give Him the throne of your heart. Cultivate your relationship with Jesus. Jeremiah 29:11 says that He has a good plan for your life, *"For I know the thoughts I think toward you"*, says the LORD, *"Thoughts of peace and not of evil, to give you a hope and a future."* Follow His plan.

Remember …

- God has a plan for your life and it is revealed in His Word.
- As you focus on Jesus and read the Bible, you are being transformed by the renewal of your mind.
- Get to know God. Do not be content to hear stories about Him, invest time *knowing* Him.
- Everything we need for life and godliness is found in Christ. He is sufficient for every situation we encounter, including deliverance from addictive thinking and behavior.
- You are a new creation in Christ and you have a totally new identity in Him. Begin acting like a new man in Christ rather than continuing to act like the person you were before you became a Christian.

Get on the road to Calvary. Stay off the road to Timnah.

Here are some Foundational Verses you can apply from this lesson ...

The thief does not come except to steal, and to kill, and to destroy. I have come that they may have life, and that they may have it more abundantly. John 10:10

But each one is tempted when he is drawn away by his own desires and enticed. Then, when desire has conceived, it gives birth to sin; and sin, when it is full-grown, brings forth death. James 1:14-15

But now having been set free from sin, and having become slaves of God, you have your fruit to holiness, and the end, everlasting life. For the wages of sin is death, but the gift of God is eternal life in Christ Jesus our Lord. Romans 6:22-23

You are going beyond addictions to live free in Christ Jesus! Congratulations on your new beginning. Continue reading your Bible every day. The Lord is doing a good work in your life. As it says in Galatians 6:9, *And let us not grow weary while doing good, for in due season we shall reap if we do not lose heart.*

In chapter 4, you will see addiction for what it really is—idolatry.

Pray as you read and ask the Lord to show you any idols that you may be harboring in your heart. Underline the points that directly address your life and apply them today. As the Holy Spirit teaches you, you will be inspired to share this message with others who can benefit from living free in Jesus Christ too.

Addiction as Idolatry

Chapter 4

You don't have to go to heathen lands today to find false gods, America is full of them. Whatever you love more than God is your idol.

D.L. Moody

In the previous chapter we looked briefly at how we descended into addiction. We moved from friendship with the sinful activity to infatuation and from there to love and betrayal. Finally, the substance or activity that we had once used was now using us; it became the center of our lives, and without realizing, we had begun to worship it.

In this lesson, we will see if addiction is a form of idolatry.

Millions of people worship idols. They purchase little statues from peddlers, take them home and bow down to the gods that they represent. It is estimated that there are at least 300,000 Hindu gods, some promise healing of various diseases; others are for rain, some for protection from evil spirits. All of them are false. You and I are much too smart to fall for something like that. Right?

Let me ask you a few questions. Have you ever purchased cocaine, methamphetamines or some other drug from a dealer on a street corner? Have you ever sought pleasure in a back alley or a cheap hotel room? Have you ever bought a porn magazine in a convenience store? Were you seeking something from your addiction that you did not believe you could get through a relationship with God? Guess what? You may have purchased an idol from a street peddler.

Even if you never bought your pleasure on the street, you may still be guilty of worshipping an idol. A former *Beyond Addictions* graduate told me, "My greatest idol was the lust for control. I hated to feel powerless or inadequate. I feel vulnerable when I'm not in control, but with God's help I am learning to submit to the leading of the Holy Spirit. Then I am free from the need to control the circumstances around me." The lust for control, or any other stronghold, can become an idol.

Dr. Edward Welch describes idolatry as "anything on which we set our affections and indulge as an excessive and sinful attachment. Therefore, the idols that we can see – such as a bottle – are certainly not the whole problem. Idolatry includes anything we worship: the lust for pleasure, respect, love, power, control, or freedom from pain. ... The problem is not the idolatrous substance; it is the false worship of the heart."[5]

Dr. Welch provides us with an important connection between addiction and idolatry. Addictive substances, thoughts and activities promise you benefits that they do not deliver. They are false gods. The problem did not begin with the bottle of beer, the marijuana joint or the pornographic picture. The problem started in our heart where we sought a source for pleasure or a solution to a problem such as our need for love, power, control, or freedom from pain. So the addiction started with false worship in our heart. It was idolatry.

Dr. Welch wasn't the first person to consider idolatry something more than the worship of little statues. In the Bible, God spoke to Ezekiel and through the Apostle Paul about the same issue. Much later, in the sixteenth century, John Calvin described man's heart as an idol factory. Fallen man constantly seeks sinful solutions to his problems and constantly fabricates idols that promise to lead him out of the darkness of his current situations, whatever they may be.

In that sense, we have worshipped drugs, alcohol, sexual pleasure, people, power and money as the solutions to the problems in our lives. All of these little idols fall down to one larger one in the life of an unbeliever. If you do not have a relationship with Jesus Christ, then the greatest idol in your life is ... you. Think about it. All addictions focus on providing some perceived benefit that you believe you need or deserve or simply crave. Addiction is all about self. Addicts of all makes and models routinely sacrifice the concerns of others in order to indulge themselves.

Let's look at a couple of scripture passages that provide a better understanding of addiction and idolatry.

---

[5] Edward T. Welch, *Addictions: A Banquet in the Grave* (Phillipsburg: P&R Publishing Company, 2001), 49.

> *And we know that the Son of God is come, and hath given us an understanding, that we may know him that is true; and we are in him that is true, even his Son Jesus Christ. This is the true God, and eternal life. Little children, keep yourselves from idols. I John 5:20-21*

Was John referring to little statues when he mentioned idols in this passage? Probably not. Look at the context of this verse. John was talking about the knowledge of God that He has given us, "… that we may know Him that is true, and we are in Him that is true, even His Son Jesus Christ. This is the true God and eternal life." Then he warns us to stay away from idols. Why? Idols cloud our understanding of the truth and interfere with our worship of God. An idol is anything that exalts itself against the knowledge of God or that interferes with our worship of Him.

John's description of the problem with idols clearly relates to addictions. They cloud your understanding and take your eyes off of God. You could use the same language as John and say, "Little children, keep yourselves from addictive activities, thoughts and substances."

Do all idols have a physical form, or can they be a habit or just a pattern of thinking? Take a look at what God tells Ezekiel about the priests who were left in Jerusalem during the early part of the Babylonian captivity.

> *Son of man, these men have set up their idols <u>in their heart</u>, and put the stumbling block of their iniquity before their face. Should I be inquired of at all by them? Ezekiel 14:3*

God told Ezekiel that idols can be set up in the heart. They are not always physical, tangible things. You can harbor lust, pornography, memories of times when you were high on drugs and other thoughts in your mind. If you do, then just like the priests in Ezekiel, you are harboring idols in your heart. Your worship of these idols interferes with your relationship with God. On this basis, God says, "Should I be inquired of at all by them?" By continuing to indulge in worshipping the idol, you are separating yourself further and further from the Lord, and you are placing yourself at great risk of actively engaging in that old addiction.

The Apostle Paul uses the failures of the Old Testament Israelites to warn Christians not to fall into idolatry.

In I Corinthians 10:6-14, Paul sites four examples of failure that occurred during the wilderness period after the Israelites were delivered from Egypt. He uses these examples essentially to say "don't let this happen to you."

> *Now these things became our examples, to the intent that we should not lust after evil things as they also lusted. And do not become idolaters as were some of them. As it is written, "The people sat down to eat and drink, and rose up to play." Nor let us commit sexual immorality, as some of them did, and in one day twenty-three thousand fell; nor let us tempt Christ, as some of them also tempted, and were destroyed by serpents; nor complain, as some of them also complained, and were destroyed by the destroyer. Now all these things happened to them as examples, and they were written for our admonition, upon whom the ends of the ages have come. Therefore let him who thinks he stands take heed lest he fall. I Corinthians 10:6-12*

First of all, Paul says that their failures were rooted in lust. They wanted something that they did not believe God was providing them. Think about it. This is still the root cause of our failures too. Maybe you were hungering for fulfillment, joy, peace or excitement. Or maybe you were desperate to have someone love you. If Satan can convince you that God is not sufficient to meet these needs, then he can trick you into a sinful solution of his own making. He scratches a lust that you harbor in your heart, and it festers into full blown sin.

Paul lists four specific examples of their failure. He is speaking to you and me too.

1) In verse 7 he refers to their worship of the golden calf in the wilderness, "And do not become idolaters as were some of them." Believing that God had left them, they returned to the way of life that they

had known in Egypt. They made a golden calf and worshipped it as god.

Sometimes you may be tempted to think that God doesn't care or that He isn't paying attention either. You lost your job. You are being accused of something that you didn't do. Your family doesn't seem to care. At these moments, you may want to go back to your old way of life when you supposedly had everything under control. Like the Israelites, you have forgotten that you were actually in bondage in your old life. Stop and think. God has not forgotten you, and He has not forsaken you. He has forgiven you. He loves you and He is in control, working all things together for good to those who love Him and are called according to His purpose (Romans 8:28).

    2)   Verse 8 mentions their fall to sexual immorality with the Moabite women, "Nor let us commit sexual immorality, as some of them did, and in one day twenty-three thousand fell." The account in Numbers 25:1-18 tells us that this also led them into idolatry. Balaam knew how to get the Israelites to worship the false gods of Moab. He did it by tempting them to commit sexual immorality with the Moabite women. Once the Israelite men were in bed with them, they began to take on the Moabites' sinful way of life.

The same thing still happens today. If you fall to sexual immorality, Satan will begin to drag you into whatever lifestyle the other person is leading. He may also tell you to go ahead and sin it up. Since you have already broken one commandment, you might as well break them all. So he tempts, he condemns you for your failure, and he drags you into further sin.

    3)   Verse 9 refers to the time when the Israelites complained about God's provision for them in Numbers 21:5, "And the people spoke against God and against Moses, 'Why have you brought us up out of Egypt to die in the wilderness? For there is no food and no water, and our soul loathes this worthless bread.'" Dissatisfied with God's provision, they complained against the very God who delivered them from slavery in Egypt. They had forgotten God's past deliverance, His protection from the Egyptian army, His provision of water from a rock, and they hated the manna that He had rained down from heaven. Our memory can be very selective and very poor too. If Satan can cause you to be dissatisfied with your current situation, then he can tempt you to seek deliverance from someone other than God. Dissatisfaction often

comes when you compare your situation with someone else whom you believe has it much better. They may have more money or a bigger house or better health. When things have been tight financially, I have been tempted to complain when I saw people at church who had plenty of money and didn't seem to have a care in the world. The Holy Spirit chastised me by saying, "What are you lacking? You don't know what they are going through in their house. Just because they have plenty of money doesn't mean that they don't have any problems." Since the Lord corrected me on this point, I have not envied anyone's financial wealth. Be satisfied with God's provisions.

4)   Verse 10 refers to a time in Numbers 16 when Korah rebelled against God and complained that Moses had taken too much authority. As a result, God showed the people of Israel whom He had appointed by destroying Korah, Dathan, Abiram and the princes of Israel who joined them in the rebellion. Rather than seeing this as God's corrective judgment, the people of Israel murmured even more against the authority of God and of Moses. As a result, God brought a plague into the camp of the Israelites and fourteen thousand people lost their lives. Rebellion against God's authority can cause people to seek solutions to their problems from other sources or to rebel against God in other ways. Some choose drugs, others alcohol, some get lost in porn or sexual perversion. Some just decide to grab the reins of power so they can control the events of their lives. All of these solutions are rooted in lust and rebellion, and they lead to destruction in the end.

With these four examples in mind, Paul tells us to watch out,

> *Therefore let him who thinks he stands take heed lest he fall. No temptation has overtaken you except such as is common to man; but God is faithful, who will not allow you to be tempted beyond what you are able, but with the temptation will also make the way of escape, that you may be able to bear it. I Corinthians 10:13*

No one is immune to temptation. If you think that you are standing on your own, watch out, you may be in for a fall. When we are tempted, Paul encourages us to look for the way of escape that God alone provides. Note this, when you are tempted, God is for you. He is trying to show you a way of escape so that you will not fall into sin.

The last thing that Paul says is the most important point for us to remember.

Therefore, my beloved, flee from idolatry.
I Corinthians 10:14

This is the clear solution to the problems Paul listed in the previous verses. Take Paul's counsel. When you think that God has departed from you, or you are tempted to fall into sin, flee idolatry rather than giving in to it. When Satan, your enemy, tempts you to be dissatisfied with God's provision or with His authority, then flee idolatry rather than trying to create a god who will better fulfill your desires. Do not look for false gods that you believe will suit you better. Do not look to false gods for deliverance. Seek the face of God in prayer; pour out your heart to Him. False gods may promise love and acceptance or relief from the trouble, but these are false promises that lead to addiction and destruction.

How can we recognize this problem and deal with it before temptations become sin and lead to idolatry?
Dr. Welch provides a description of the early and later stages of addiction that help us to recognize when idols in the making are disguised as seemingly little sins or indulgencies.

"In the early stages of addiction, we were in rebellion. Our heart desired just one more and our body was briefly satisfied. ... Then, in later stages, we were in bondage. Our idolatrous hearts wanted more but when we received it, our physical desires were not met and demanded more!"[6]

In the early stages, it's like eating chocolate candy. One or two after a meal and your desire for sweets is satisfied. It's a nice treat after a meal. No big deal. Right?

In a later stage you look for a chocolate or two after lunch and dinner. Suddenly, you are making sure that you always have a bag of chocolate around the house and you look for a handful after every meal. Without your "sweet treat," the meal is not complete and you are not

---

[6] Ibid., 52.

satisfied. Soon you are stopping for a mid-morning break … and another one in the middle of the afternoon. Your little desire for a sweet treat has gotten out of control, and it now controls you.

The "chocolate" analogy looks pretty lame compared to the type of addiction you have dealt with; however, the principles are probably the same. You started with a taste for something that provided a little pleasure and it led to taking a lot just to alleviate the pain. Soon the "sweet treat" had set up shop in the middle of your heart and demanded attention. It became an idol. Your sweet treat may have been drug use that started as a weekend retreat then became necessary to get you through every day. It may have been a phone call to a married friend of the opposite sex, and it became an affair that you did not know how to get out of. Whatever it was, it was easier to stop in the early stage of rebellion than in the later stage of bondage and addiction.

The best advice is to nip the problem in the bud. If you garden, you know that small weeds are a lot easier to remove than big ones, that a little attention to the problem early on and every day will help you avoid having your beautiful garden destroyed when the weeds take over the place. Use the four issues in I Corinthians 10 as early warning weed detectors. These four warnings will enable you to take inventory in your heart and find out if there is any seed of rebellion that needs to be addressed. Are there any small weeds growing in your garden? Take the time to uproot them. You will be glad you did.

Does God really consider these sinful desires to be idolatry?

Idolatry is a pretty serious charge. To be guilty of idol worship means that you have forsaken Jesus Christ in order to get something you need or want from another god. Is coveting the same as idolatry? To covet means that you only desire these things in your heart. You haven't even taken action on them … yet. I mean, is it really so bad to want love and acceptance from a woman you're not married to? Or to fantasize about things that God has not provided? What about all of those memories of drug use or drunkenness, are they really so bad? After all, isn't that better than actively using them? Does God really consider a little covetousness as idolatry?

What does the Bible say? In at least two scripture passages, God says that covetousness is a form of idolatry.

For this you know, that no fornicator, unclean person, nor covetous man, <u>who is an idolater</u>, has any inheritance in the kingdom of Christ and God. Ephesians 5:5

Therefore put to death your members which are on the earth: fornication, uncleanness, passion, evil desire, and <u>covetousness, which is idolatry.</u> Colossians 3:5

The Greek word translated "covetous" in Ephesians 5:5 means "desiring more, eager for gain." So a person who is eager for personal gain is an idolater. This sounds like the problem that Korah and the boys had in Numbers 16. Watch out for this idol in your heart. When you are dissatisfied with your wife or your financial situation, you are being set up to fall to a false god that offers a better deal. In reality, you will eventually be in bondage.

The word translated as "covetous" in Colossians 3:5 means "avarice, greediness." It is the same word used in Luke 12:15 when Jesus said, *Take heed and beware of covetousness, for one's life does not consist in the abundance of the things he possesses.* In other words, life isn't about the stuff. When we get our eyes focused on the pleasures of this world, we become confused. We become dissatisfied with God and His provisions, and we seek to fulfill our covetous desires in some other way. According to Ephesians 5:5 and Colossians 3:5, this is idolatry.

So you can see how subtly our wrong desires can lead to sin, rebellion, idolatry and bondage to addiction. This is true about illegal addictions like drugs, as well as the ones that may not be illegal but are extremely harmful to us personally and against God's perfect will for our lives.

How can we avoid this problem?

First of all, Colossians 3:5 tells us that we are not to tame our lusts; we are supposed to put them to death, to separate ourselves from them. Doing drugs less often or smoking marijuana rather than crack isn't the answer. Don't let the enemy trick you into thinking that you can control your sin or that a little sin is okay. It isn't.

You need to understand the seriousness of the fight in order to have hope for victory. We are not just addressing principles of putting away addictions; we are here to rid them from our lives.

Here is some Biblical counsel that will help you avoid idolatry and addiction.

1.   Focus on the One we worship. Remember that Jesus Christ is sufficient to meet our needs in every situation. Focus on Christ. The solution to idolatry is to get our eyes back on Jesus. In I Thessalonians 1:9, the believers in Thessalonica were commended because they turned to God from idols to serve the living and true God. They didn't just turn from idols. They turned towards God. Like the old hymn says, when you turn your eyes upon Jesus, the things of this world grow strangely dim in the light of His glory and grace. Remember Hebrews 12:1-2. The method and the motivation for successfully running the race is to fix your eyes on Jesus Christ, the author and finisher of your faith.

2.   Use the tools that God has provided for spiritual battle. All battles with addiction are spiritual. The power behind these thoughts and substances belongs to Satan. He has created attractive alternatives to worshipping the one true God, and we bowed to them in the past. How can we successfully fight the battle against idolatry? Use some Biblical tools:

Tool #1 Take thoughts captive. You cannot defeat spiritual enemies using earthly weapons. *For though we walk in the flesh, we do not war according to the flesh. For the weapons of our warfare are not carnal but mighty in God for pulling down strongholds, <u>casting down arguments and every high thing that exalts itself against the knowledge of God, bringing every thought into captivity to the obedience of Christ</u>. II Corinthians 10:3-5.*

Tool #2 Submit to God. *Submit yourselves therefore to God. James 4:7* As sheep, we get in trouble when we wander away from the protection of the Good Shepherd. Rebellion from God will only bring sin and pain. There is great protection in living in submission to God.

Tool #3 Resist Satan. *Resist the devil and he will flee. James 4:7* You can deal with the schemes of the enemy much easier by catching his tempting thoughts as they first enter your mind. "Get behind me, Satan. The Lord rebuke you. That thought is not from God."

Tool #4 Pray. *Draw near to God and he will draw near to you. James 4:8* This is a promise. When you move towards the Lord, He moves towards you. Pray. God is listening.

Tool #5 Use the Word of God. In Luke 4:1-13, Jesus employed the Word of God when He was tempted by Satan. He went directly to scripture to resist the devil. You should to the same.

Tool #6 Put on the full armor of God. Study each aspect of the armor that is described in Ephesians 6:12-18. 1) Have your back (loins) covered with the truth of God; when you are honest, you don't have to cover your own back, Jesus will be your rear guard.

2) Wear the breastplate of the righteousness of Jesus Christ. His righteousness is perfect. It will guard your heart just like the breastplate protected the heart of the Roman soldiers in battle.

3) Walk in the good news of Jesus Christ. When you are walking in the Word then you are not prone to fall. 4) Uphold the shield of faith as you encounter the uncertainties of life. You will not understand all of life's twists and turns; you just need to trust that the Lord is controlling them. By doing so, you will eliminate the fear and anxiety that the enemy wants you to fall victim to.

5) Think on the things of God (wear the helmet of salvation). As Paul says in Philippians 4:8, *Finally, brethren, whatever things are true, whatever things are noble, whatever things are just, whatever things are pure, whatever things are lovely, whatever things are of good report, if there is any virtue and if there is anything praiseworthy-- meditate on these things.*

6) Take the sword of the Spirit, which is the Word of God. Spend time reading God's Word, and the Holy Spirit will put it to use at the appropriate time in your life. Reading the Bible will change your life. There is no substitute in this spiritual battle for regular Bible reading and study.

7) Above all else, pray, pray, pray. *Praying always with all prayer and supplication in the Spirit, being watchful to this*

end with all perseverance and supplication for all the saints. Ephesians 6:18 Wow, it looks like Paul pretty well covered our defense in these seven verses. Put them to work.

Josiah was one of the godliest kings to rule Judah. In II Kings 23:6, King Josiah removed the idol that had been erected in the temple, burned it, stamped it to powder and threw it in the graveyard. He did not leave anything that even symbolized that old idol. How should you act upon the idols in your heart?

The Apostle Paul addresses this question in the sixth chapter of II Corinthians.

And what agreement has the temple of God with idols? For you are the temple of the living God. As God has said: "I will dwell in them And walk among them. I will be their God, And they shall be My people." Therefore "Come out from among them And be separate, says the Lord. Do not touch what is unclean, And I will receive you." II Corinthians 6:16-17

What is Paul directing you to do when he says, "touch not the unclean thing"? There are physical items that were part of your old addictions. Identify them and move them out of your life. Get rid of the bong pipes, the roach clips, needles, photos, magazines, old letters, beer signs and anything else that would lead to setting that idol back in your heart. And stay away from the places and people who are continuing in their addiction.

Paul says that you are the temple of the living God. So your call to purity in the temple of your body is the same as the call to purity in the Old Testament Temple. When you harbor idols in your heart, you are as guilty of sin as the priests mentioned in Ezekiel 14:3 who worshipped idols in God's Temple in Jerusalem.

Finally, ask the Lord regularly to do a heart-cleaning so that the idolatrous thoughts cannot set up house again in your life. King David was called a man after God's own heart. His desire expressed in Psalm 139:23-24 explains why:

Search me, Oh God, and know my heart; try me, and know my thoughts; and see if there be any wicked way in me, and lead me in the way everlasting. Psalm 139:23-24

We have covered a lot of scripture in this chapter. Hopefully, you see how seriously the Bible treats idolatry, and you understand that you had actually set up an idol in your heart when you were in addiction.

I pray that those days are past now and that you are living as a new creation in Christ Jesus. If you are still harboring any idols or if you are struggling with addiction, you need to know that God loves you and He wants to remove the idol so that you can experience the abundant life in Christ that He offers.

Review the scripture passages in this chapter. Agree with the Lord that you have a problem and ask Him to take it from you. Focus your eyes on Jesus Christ, the author and finisher of your faith. Then actively be on guard to make sure that you are not making any new idols in your life.

Finally, invite God daily to search your heart to see if there is any wicked way in you and ask Him to lead you in the way that is everlasting.

What else does the Bible say about addiction?

In the previous chapter, you saw addiction as a form of idolatry. What else does the Bible say about this problem? Would you believe that addiction is portrayed as … voluntary slavery, as adultery and ultimately as life-dominating sin? These are the three views of addiction that you will explore now. Thank God that you will also look at the solution to these problems. The solution isn't a pill or a treatment program; it's a person and His name is Jesus Christ.

Other Biblical Views of Addiction

Chapter 5

There is great power in the name of Jesus, in the blood of Jesus,
and the work of the Holy Spirit.
No one else and nothing else can cure you from sin
or keep you from temptation.

In *A Journey to Victorious Pray*ing, author Bill Thrasher tells about a student who struggled with an addictive habit:

> Jim's struggle with an ungodly habit in his life led him to cry out to God for deliverance. Nothing happened. One day a person came up and had the love and discernment to graciously confront Jim by saying, "Why are you asking God to deliver you from this ungodly habit? You love this ungodly habit. You do not really want God to answer your prayer." Jim admitted that this was precisely the truth.
>
> Jim said that one of the most humbling things he had ever done was to come to God and tell Him that he loved this ungodly habit and did not really want Him to answer his prayer for deliverance. Jim also informed me that this honest prayer was the beginning of the process of breaking him from the habit![7]

Jim had a serious problem, an ungodly habit that he could not control; it was an addiction. He approached the problem with a little prayer and continued wondering why he was still struggling with this sin. Jim hadn't gotten to the root of the problem. The root issue was that he still loved this sinful habit. It required confrontation with the truth in order for him to admit to himself and to God that he still secretly loved the ungodly habit.

---

[7] Bill Thrasher, *A Journey to Victorious Praying*, (Chicago: Moody Publishers, 2003), 27.

Does this sound familiar? If you have ever struggled with addiction, then you understand Jim's situation. Addiction is cancerous, and it will consume you if it is not removed. The Bible provides the correct diagnosis, and it offers the cure for the problem. It confronts you with the truth, reveals the motives of your heart and tells you when you are harboring sinful habits. If you are still struggling with an ungodly habit, then you may be secretly in love with the sin. If that is the case, then admit it to God and let His light shine in that hidden area of your heart. Once you admit the problem, it is easier to receive treatment and to be cured.

The Bible describes the problem of addiction in a number of ways. In the last chapter we looked at addiction as idolatry. In this chapter, we will see it described as voluntary slavery, compared with adultery and revealed as life-dominating sin. You will also see how God can release you from slavery to addiction, forgive your adultery and remove the sin that has dominated your life.

Voluntary Slavery

"Okay men, we need a few volunteers for an important mission. Who will step forward and volunteer to be enslaved by a cruel task master? Any takers? None? You mean that no one here wants to volunteer to be a slave for the rest of your life?"

We would be seriously concerned for anyone who would step forward and take this offer. Guess what. Most of us volunteered for slavery to addiction.

Why would you volunteer for slavery? Well, probably because you didn't realize what you were really volunteering for.

During the 17th and 18th centuries, many people left Europe with the promise of land and opportunity in the new world. All they would have to do is serve a landowner on his plantation for a period of seven years to receive their freedom and their earthly reward. Once they arrived on the shores of North America, they realized that they had been duped. They were indentured servants tied to a cruel taskmaster. They would spend the rest of their lives working in harsh conditions with no hope of freedom unless they could buy their way out of slavery.

Many addicts have been enslaved in similar fashion. They bought the lie that using drugs would give them freedom from pain or relief from memories of the past. Once they were under the power of the addiction, they realized that they were not free; in fact, they were more enslaved than ever with no apparent hope and no way out.

You may have become addicted the same way. You thought you were volunteering for pleasure, for relief, for ecstasy. You may have started using drugs in order to be accepted by your peers or to relieve some pain. Whatever the reason for starting the habit, you never intended to become enslaved to something that you thought you controlled.

What went wrong? First of all, you were seeking happiness through sinfulness. Satan, your enemy, sold you a bill of goods. He tells everyone that they will receive happiness through unrighteous means – sexual adultery, drunkenness, drug use, dirty movies. In John 8:44, Jesus says that Satan was a liar from the beginning and the father of lies.

Let's set the record straight. You will never receive true happiness through unrighteousness. True happiness is found as you walk in true righteousness.

> *You love righteousness and hate wickedness. Therefore God, Your God, has anointed you with the oil of gladness more than Your companions. Psalm 45:7*

The passage is a prophecy of Jesus Christ; however, the statement it makes regarding righteousness, lawlessness and happiness is also true about us. There is a direct connection between our love of righteousness, our hatred for wickedness in our hearts, and the level of happiness in our lives.

An unholy person is rarely if ever happy. Sin offers some relief or temporary pleasures but it never provides real happiness. A sinful person appears happy one moment and depressed the next. You cannot find happiness by pursuing it in pornography or drunkenness or drug use. This is true for unbelievers, and it is true for Christians. If you dabble or flirt with unrighteousness, then happiness drains out of your life.

So, Satan tricked you just like he tricks others. He told you that the way to true happiness, to get relief or to find peace was to take one of his pills or to engage in one of his schemes. In chapter 3 we looked at Satan as a fisherman; he knows the minds and habits of those he is trying to catch, and he knows just how to lure them. He baits his hook with something that promises fulfillment, excitement or relief. He attracts some men with dissatisfaction in their home life. They begin to think that their wife isn't as attractive or as exciting as she was when they first met. Satan draws them with an attractive young woman at work or the gym. At the same time, he causes her to believe that this married man is the solution to all of her problems. She becomes one attractive lure.

Satan torments others with painful memories of abuse and rejection by their parents. Then he lures them with a pain killer or a hallucinogen that provides temporary relief.

Think about your past experiences. You felt a need or a desire that wasn't being met. Satan threw something in front of you that looked like it could fill the void very nicely. At first, this lure was pretty satisfying. You were excited by this new relationship or you enjoyed some time without the pain of the past resurfacing in your mind. You were being baited. Satan is a crafty fisherman. He doesn't play "catch and release"; he wants you for life. So he drew you along until it was time to throw you some bait with a hook. It looked the same as it did before, and you swallowed it, hook, line and sinker. Then he jerked the line and you were trapped. The other woman or man was wearing a disguise; they were controlling and deceptive and began to dominate your life. You realized the ugliness of your sin but also thought that it was too late to get out of it. The drug no longer satisfied. It left a gnawing emptiness, and it took all of your income to pay for more of it.

This is how we volunteered to participate in something that would eventually enslave us. Just like a big bass, we took the bait thinking that this was just a casual lunch and didn't realize that it was for our life. We had a strong desire for it. We were tempted. We were drawn away to the evil. And we became its servant. The following scripture passages were written over 1900 years ago, and they are still true.

Jesus answered them, "Most assuredly, I say to you, whoever commits sin is a slave of sin." John 8:34

The Bible tells me that if I practice sin, then I am a slave to that sin. It isn't serving me; I am serving it!

We never thought of ourselves as slaves to sin, but the Bible says that is what we were before Jesus Christ set us free from sinful attachments. We thought that we controlled our own sin. Nope, the Bible says that it controlled us, and we served it.

> *Blessed is the man who endures temptation; for when he has been approved, he will receive the crown of life which the Lord has promised to those who love Him. Let no one say when he is tempted, "I am tempted by God"; for God cannot be tempted by evil, nor does He Himself tempt anyone. But each one is tempted when he is drawn away by his own desires and enticed. Then, when desire has conceived, it gives birth to sin; and sin, when it is full-grown, brings forth death. James 1:12-15*

James 1:12-15 provides a classic description of a fish taking the bait. It says that each one of us is tempted when we are drawn away by our own lust and enticed. Where does the lust come from? We harbored it in our hearts. Who does the enticing? Satan, the fisherman. Then the desire conceived, and we took action on the temptation. That is when we fell into sin. Initially, the bait provided some satisfaction, but there was no hook in it yet. Satan was just playing us until the right time. The result of falling into sin is death. Death literally means separation. For all of us, addiction resulted in separation from God. For some people it led to physical death. In all cases, the lure did not satisfy very long and it came with a hook that we didn't expect.

For a time, we voluntarily used the bait (those thoughts, people, pictures, activities and substances) for our own momentary pleasure. The satisfaction was enticing, and there didn't seem to be any serious consequences. When the hook was set, we were slaves to these sinful attachments, and they controlled our lives. We had volunteered for slavery.

Remember this illustration, and remember how foolish it looks to volunteer for something that will eventually bind you as a slave. According to John 10:10, Satan wants to kill you, steal from you and destroy you. He did not come to give you a good time; he came to enslave you, and to take your life. On the other hand, Jesus says in the same verse that He wants to give you abundant life. He came to set you free. John 8:36 says, *Therefore if the Son makes you free, you shall be free indeed.* He doesn't bait you with one thing and enslave you with something else. He came to set you free from sin and to give you real life, abundant life.

Satan will often tempt you with short cuts that appear to fulfill your desires, but they don't and they come with serious side effects. Think about the men who left Europe believing in the false promise of freedom and opportunity. Many of them spent their lives in slavery. Some were able to purchase their freedom after years of service. There were also many men who were enticed by the offer to serve seven years for land and freedom but didn't take the bait. Instead, they waited in Europe until they saved their money and entered the new world as free men. Their patience paid off in freedom and opportunity. They avoided the trap. This is good advice for you and me. Avoid the trap of slavery to addiction that is often hidden behind the promise of easy returns or short cuts to happiness or pleasure, "All you have to do is take this pill and your problems will be solved." "What you need is a weekend on the wild side."

I pray that you are now free from slavery to addiction. If so, take the following advice:

> *Stand fast therefore in the liberty by which Christ has made us free, and do not be entangled again with a yoke of bondage. Galatians 5:1*

Stand fast, persevere, and remain stationary in the freedom that Jesus Christ has given you. Continue reading the Bible and ask the Holy Spirit for guidance to understand it. Admit your weaknesses and ask the Lord for His help. Invite the Holy Spirit to remove the lust in your heart so that you will not be entangled in the sinful addiction again. Stay away from the thoughts, activities and places where you were once enticed. If you do not take the bait, you cannot be hooked.

Adultery

Adultery in marriage is a serious betrayal between husband and wife. God wants you to understand that it is just as serious between a

Christian, who is part of the bride of Christ, and our bridegroom Jesus Christ. According to the Bible, departing from the true and living God in order to find satisfaction from another is adultery.

How can someone be guilty of committing adultery against the Lord? God has designed marriage in such a way that we derive satisfaction from our spouse. If we seek to be satisfied emotionally or sexually through a relationship with someone other than our spouse, then we have committed adultery. Jesus even says that when a man lusts *in his heart*, he has committed adultery (Matthew 5:28). In other words, we can create a sinful attachment with someone other than our spouse and be guilty of adultery even though we have not engaged in a sexual act with that person. The sin begins in the heart. In the same way, we committed spiritual adultery when we sought satisfaction through thoughts, activities or use of a substance rather than being satisfied with Jesus. Our attempts to be fulfilled in sinful ways were acts of adultery against the Lord. They were just as serious as an act of adultery between husband and wife.

God compares the serious sin of idolatry to adultery in a number of Old Testament scriptures. He uses this comparison to describe the sinfulness of Israel and the reason for His judgment against them.

> *Then I saw that for all the causes for which backsliding Israel had committed adultery, I had put her away and given her a certificate of divorce; yet her treacherous sister Judah did not fear, but went and played the harlot also. So it came to pass, through her casual harlotry, that she defiled the land and committed adultery with stones and trees.*
> *Jeremiah 3:8-9*

> *For they have committed adultery, and blood is on their hands. They have committed adultery with their idols, and even sacrificed their sons whom they bore to Me, passing them through the fire, to devour them. (Referring to the people of Israel before the Babylonian captivity.)*
> *Ezekiel 23:37*

In these two passages, God says that when Israel worshipped idols, they were committing adultery against Him. He uses the awful sin of adultery to help us understand the evilness and wickedness of idolatry.

Anytime we put another god before our Lord, we, as the Bride of Christ, are also committing adultery. Have you ever noticed that drug and alcohol addiction are often accompanied by sexual immorality? It is also true that sexual immorality often leads to addiction to drugs, alcohol or pornography. This isn't a coincidence. There is a spiritual connection between sexual sin and other forms of addiction.

Take a look at the consequences of spiritual adultery. The people of Judah that Jeremiah and Ezekiel were addressing lost their homes; many lost their lives and most were taken captive by the Babylonians. If we choose to continue in idolatrous, adulterous sin, then we will face the consequences of our decisions too. For some, it is the loss of their family, for others it may be prison. Whatever the case, addiction to sinful attachments, thoughts or activities carries an awful price.

There is an interesting account in Proverbs 7:1-27 where an alluring woman tempts a young man to commit adultery. It sheds some light on how we were lured into a relationship with someone or something that was equally as sinful and separated us from our Lord for a time:

> *My son, keep my words, And treasure my commands within you. Keep my commands and live, and my law as the apple of your eye. Bind them on your fingers; Write them on the tablet of your heart. Say to wisdom, "You are my sister," And call understanding your nearest kin, that they may keep you from the immoral woman, from the seductress who flatters with her words.   Proverbs 7:1-5*

Solomon, the author, encourages us to abide in God's Word, to keep it close to our eyes, to wrap it around our fingers and to write it on our heart. God's Word provides discernment that keeps us from being lured by seductive women or men who flatter with their words. You can also be seduced by booze or dope or anything else that lures you into its trap.

> *For at the window of my house I looked through my lattice, And saw among the simple, I perceived among the*

youths, A young man devoid of understanding, passing along the street near her corner; And he took the path to her house in the twilight, in the evening, In the black and dark night. And there a woman met him, with the attire of a harlot, and a crafty heart. She was loud and rebellious. Her feet would not stay at home. At times she was outside, at times in the open square, Lurking at every corner. So she caught him and kissed him. With an impudent face she said to him: "I have peace offerings with me. Today I have paid my vows. So I came out to meet you, diligently to seek your face. And I have found you. Proverbs 7:6-15

This sounds like the stuff that Hollywood movies are made of. This guy is going to have a little romantic tryst with an older married woman. Many unbelievers dream about this sort of thing. A lot of men and women have become involved in extramarital affairs to get a little excitement or to have a little thrill; however, you need to look at the results. You will never receive true happiness through unrighteousness. This foolish young man is wandering in places where he shouldn't go and responds to the call of a harlot. He is risking more than he realizes as he allows himself to pursue a little excitement through a sinful relationship.

The alluring woman caught him, kissed him, flattered him and made him an offer that *looked* too good to refuse. Sin looks good on the surface, but it never supplies all that it promises, and it comes with side effects that may cost your life.

With her enticing speech she caused him to yield, with her flattering lips she seduced him. Immediately he went after her, as an ox goes to the slaughter, Or as a fool to the correction of the stocks, till an arrow struck his liver. As a bird hastens to the snare, He did not know it would cost his life. Proverbs 7:21-23

"With her enticing speech" she caused him to yield. She flattered him and lured him into her net. Your first experience with drugs, booze or sex came with enticing speech. It promised acceptance with your peers, excitement and pleasure. It's interesting that it did not come with a warning label stating that it was addictive, would cost more than you ever wanted to pay, would make you sick in the morning, might ruin your marriage, etc. The addictive stuff looked good. Like this unsuspecting youth, you went after it all the way. You didn't realize that you were going as an ox to be slaughtered, and you did not see what was coming until a dart had struck you in the liver. That is the part that usually gets left out of the movies. There are serious consequences to sin.

The chapter ends with tragedy and a warning.

> *Now therefore, listen to me, my children; Pay attention to the words of my mouth: Do not let your heart turn aside to her ways, Do not stray into her paths; for she has cast down many wounded, And all who were slain by her were strong men. Her house is the way to hell, descending to the chambers of death. Proverbs 7:24-27*

Wait a minute! You probably thought her house was the way to pleasure, and that Internet porn sight would give you a little thrill. You thought the dope and booze would *add* something to life. Guess what? You and I were wrong! Proverbs 7:25-27 says that it all leads to death.

We are fortunate. Many who have gone into the depths of addiction never came out. By God's grace, we have been given another chance and a new life in Christ Jesus. Knowing what we know now, we would do well to listen to this warning in Proverbs and stay away from the alluring sin that might entice us into a deadly trap.

Fortunately, God also offers hope for those who have committed idolatry and adultery against Him. The entire book of Hosea deals with a man who was married to a harlot. She continued in sin, selling herself on the street, and miraculously, he continued loving her. Eventually, she was used up and sold by her master. Then Hosea made a supreme act of love and grace; he paid the price to buy her out of whoredom. He forgave her and restored her as his bride. This is a picture of God's grace for the nation of Israel, and for us as lost souls who were caught up in the cares of this idolatrous, adulterous world.

Jesus paid the price to buy us out of whoredom to sin. He rescued us and made a way for us to be set free from its bondage. The price was high; it cost His life but He willingly paid it to bring us out of our adultery, to wash us clean and forgive us. So your spiritual adultery has been completely forgiven by the blood of Jesus. All you have to do is admit your sin, repent and ask Jesus to forgive you. AMEN.

Life-dominating Sins

Remember what Jesus said about sin in John 8:34, *Most assuredly, I say to you, whoever commits sin is a slave of sin.* Slavery isn't a part-time occupation; it is constant forced servitude. As a slave to addiction, you were constantly forced to serve it. It was sinful and it dominated your life.

Remember Dr. Welch's definition of addiction as *bondage* to the rule of a substance, activity, or state of mind, *which then becomes the center of life,* defending itself from the truth so that even bad consequences don't bring repentance, and *leading to further estrangement from God.* Addiction is sinful. It brings you into bondage, becomes the center of your life, and it leads to further estrangement from God.[8] It is a sinful attachment that dominates your life.

The Biblical Counseling Foundation's *Self-Confrontation: A Manual for In-Depth Biblical Discipleship* has this to say about addiction:

> When you willingly or unknowingly are under the control of any power other than God's Holy Spirit (e.g. drugs, alcohol, sex, another person, your peer group, a false religion, a self-centered habit such as gossip or laziness, or a self-oriented desire for power, food or wealth) you are in bondage to sin. However God has broken the power of sin through the Lord Jesus Christ, and you can overcome sinful habits by depending on His strength and being obedient to His Word.[9]

The authors of *Self-Confrontation* call addictions what they are; they refer to them as life-dominating sins.[10] John C. Broger developed this manual to enable Christians to examine our lives to see if

---

[8] Edward T. Welch, *Addictions: A Banquet in the Grave*, (Phillipsburg: P&R Publishing Company, 2001).

[9] John C. Broger, *Self-Confrontation: A Manual for In-Depth Biblical Discipleship*, (Palm Desert: Biblical Counseling Foundation, 1991).

[10] Ibid.

we are truly living what we say we believe. Mr. Broger was a devout Christian who served for twenty-three years as a civilian officer in the Pentagon with the United States Joint Chiefs of Staff. Following his retirement in 1977, he developed the Self-Confrontation manual. It is a rich resource that provides scriptural direction for real change. In one part of this manual, Mr. Broger provides a guide to help you determine if you are entertaining life-dominating sins. If you examine your heart and find that there are thoughts or actions that can be described by more than a few of these statements, then you can identify them as addictions or life-dominating sins.

1. You practice this sin even though you have tried repeatedly to stop.
2. You practice this sin and blame others or circumstances for your failure to stop.
3. You deny that what you are doing is sin.
4. You convince yourself that you are not enslaved to this sin and "can stop at any time" even though you continue in this sin.
5. You convince yourself that this sin has no power over you since you do not commit this sin as much as you once did.
6. You repeat the sin even though any pleasure or satisfaction to yourself is short-lived while the harm to yourself and others is considerable and long term.
7. You seek to hide your sin.
8. You revile or slander the very people who are seeking to restore you to the Lord and others.
9. You continue in this sin although you know that it is not edifying to do so.
10. You still commit this sin although you know that it obscures the testimony of Jesus Christ in your life and is a stumbling block to others.
11. You continue in this sin despite the knowledge that God's Word tells you to stop sinning and that God's provisions are sufficient to release you from this bondage.
12. You repeatedly commit this sin while knowing that this does not please the Lord nor bring glory to God.

13.   You continue in this sin even though you realize that your
       deeds (thoughts, words and actions) do not conform to the
       character of Christ.[11]

That's quite a list. Take a good look at it. Do you recognize any
sinful attachments in your life that fit these descriptions? If so, then you
are already entertaining life-dominating sins (addictions), or you are at
risk of doing so. Thinking back to the last chapter, you will also recognize these sinful attachments as idols that you are beginning to form in
your heart.

What is the solution to this problem?

It begins with the sacrifice made by Jesus Christ that redeemed you
and me from our sin. The prophecy of our Savior in Isaiah 53:5-6 says
that we were healed when he took the punishment for our sin.

> *But He was wounded for our transgressions, He was
> bruised for our iniquities; The chastisement for our peace
> was upon Him, And by His stripes we are healed. All we
> like sheep have gone astray; We have turned, every one, to
> his own way; And the LORD has laid on Him the iniquity of
> us all. Isaiah 53:5-6*

The cure for addiction and all sin is found in the shed blood, death
and resurrection of Jesus. Apart from Jesus Christ, we are powerless to
be cured. We may trade one addiction for another (drugs, alcohol,
overeating, violence, smoking, sex, etc.), but we are powerless to overcome without Him.

Jesus Christ can set you free from the sin that once dominated your
life. There have been many times as I have struggled with temptation or
with thoughts from the past that I have prayed and simply thanked God
for the blood of Jesus that has cleansed me from all sin. I could not
seem to wrestle the temptation to the ground nor outrun it, but I could
thank Jesus for the blood that forgave my sin. At that moment, I knew
that I was forgiven and that Satan has no hold on me anymore. As I
continue to submit my life to the leading of the Holy Spirit, I continue
to have victory over sin.

---

[11] Ibid.

There is great power in the name of Jesus, in the blood of Jesus, and the work of the Holy Spirit. No one else and nothing else can cure you from sin or keep you from temptation.

Conclusion

If you are like me, you probably see your past reflected in this chapter and the two previous ones we have studied – we entered into voluntary slavery and adultery; we were dominated by sin. Thank God that does not have to be the case any longer because Jesus Christ has not only provided the solution; He is the solution.

I pray that you have emerged from the cloud of addiction and realize that what you were doing was an offence against God. You need to know that in spite of your sin and rebellion, God still loves you so much that He made a way for your sins to be forgiven and your life to be redeemed. Jesus provided the way through His own blood and sacrificial death for sin to be removed. When God's wrath was poured out on Jesus at the cross, He took the wrath that you and I deserved. His resurrection from the grave proved that the price paid in His blood was sufficient to redeem and forgive us. We are forgiven. Now we know that if we confess our sin to the Lord and ask for His forgiveness, He is faithful and just to forgive us and to cleanse us from all unrighteousness (I John 1:9). We are free to live a new life in Jesus Christ.

Now that you are free, do not let those old sins come back into your life. Prayerfully examine your lifestyle and open your heart to the conviction of the Holy Spirit. Like David prayed in Psalm 139, ask the Lord to search your heart and mind, to see if there is any wicked way in you, and lead you in the way that is everlasting. See if there are any ungodly habits that you may have tried to give up to God in prayer but are still secretly in love with. Admit your weakness to God. This may be the beginning of being set free from this sin that plagues your life. Praise God that He IS the cure for all of our ills, even the ones that are self-inflicted. He came to set us free. And he whom the Son sets free is free indeed!

Foundational Scriptures to consider …

Therefore, if anyone is in Christ, he is a new creation; old things have passed away; behold, all things have become new. II Corinthians 5:17

The thief does not come except to steal, and to kill, and to destroy. I have come that they may have life, and that they may have it more abundantly. John 10:10

Or do you not know that your body is the temple of the Holy Spirit who is in you, whom you have from God, and you are not your own? For you were bought at a price; therefore glorify God in your body and in your spirit, which are God's. I Corinthians 6:19-20

But each one is tempted when he is drawn away by his own desires and enticed. Then, when desire has conceived, it gives birth to sin; and sin, when it is full-grown, brings forth death. James 1:14-15

Then He said to them all, "If anyone desires to come after Me, let him deny himself, and take up his cross daily, and follow Me. "For whoever desires to save his life will lose it, but whoever loses his life for My sake will save it. Luke 9:23-24

Therefore lay aside all filthiness and overflow of wickedness, and receive with meekness the implanted word, which is able to save your souls. But be doers of the word, and not hearers only, deceiving your-selves. James 1:21-22

Part III

Biblical Solutions to the Problem of Addiction

That I May Know Him
Jesus Christ is Sufficiency for All Things
Your New Identity in Christ
Making the Change

The book is entitled *Beyond Addictions*, not just *Addictions*. My prayer is that you will move beyond what has enslaved you and held you in bondage. Having looked at the issue of addiction, it is time to look directly into the face of the One who defeated addiction, and enabled you and me to live free and abundant lives.

Many of us tried to avoid God in our attempt to get past drugs, alcohol or abusive behavior. We were willing to try anything except God to be free from addiction. It wasn't a very wise plan.

In this chapter, you will get to know God in ways that you may never have known Him before. You will see Him as your nourisher and strength-giver. You will see Him as the One who provides and heals, as the merciful and gracious God who is revealed in the face of Jesus Christ.

That I May Know Him

Chapter 6

"The gruesome, exhausting, trouble-filled life that I once lived is over.
It ended when I decided to follow Jesus with my whole heart. I don't
carry the burdens of drug addiction anymore.
Jesus took the burdens away."
V. R. – *Beyond Addictions* Graduate 2010

The problems of addiction are not solved by focusing on the addiction. They are solved by focusing on Jesus Christ and allowing the Holy Spirit to take charge of your life. You know that addiction can be an all-consuming problem. I want you to understand that the solution is much bigger; His name is Jesus.

The Apostle Paul had been following Jesus for thirty years when he wrote the following. Pay particular attention to the underlined passages:

> *Yet indeed I also count all things loss for the excellence of the knowledge of Christ Jesus my Lord, for whom I have suffered the loss of all things, and count them as rubbish, that I may gain Christ and be found in Him, not having my own righteousness, which is from the law, but that which is through faith in Christ, the righteousness which is from God by faith; that I may know Him and the power of His resurrection, and the fellowship of His sufferings, being conformed to His death if, by any means, I may attain to the resurrection from the dead. ... Brethren, I do not count myself to have apprehended; but one thing I do, forgetting those things which are behind and reaching forward to those things which are ahead, I press toward the goal for the prize of the upward call of God in Christ Jesus. Philippians 3:8-11, 13-14*

After 30 years with Jesus, Paul still wanted to know Him more. It was his passion; it was the goal of his life. More than serving Jesus, Paul wanted to know Jesus.

Pastor Chuck Smith of Calvary Chapel of Costa Mesa often says that all men are created with a "God-shaped vacuum." All of us have an emptiness inside that can only be filled by God. Man was created by God to worship Him and to fellowship with Him, and it is through a relationship with God that we are fulfilled. This was the focus of life for the Apostle Paul and as a result, he lived a very full and fulfilling life. By seeking to know God, your life will be very rewarding too.

Real life

Jesus talked about the importance of our relationship with Him. Speaking to the Father, He said,

> *And this is eternal life, that they may know You, the on-ly true God, and Jesus Christ whom You have sent. John 17:3*

Eternal life begins when we are born again and start to know Jesus Christ. Jesus said that this is real life. As you will see in this chapter, we come to know God the Father through the revelation of Jesus Christ, His only Son, and this revelation is contained in His autobiography – the Bible.

Why is all of this important to someone who has struggled with addiction? Our problems were rooted, at least in part, in our attempts to fill this "God-shaped vacuum" with something other than a relation-ship with God. We tried pills; we tried sexual pleasure; we tried just about everything that the world threw at us to fill the emptiness. It was the focus of our life. God promises us something that doesn't just tem-porarily take away the emptiness; He fills us eternally and abundantly!

In the Book of John, Jesus compares all other claims of this world to His own offer of satisfaction. He says,

> *The thief does not come except to steal, and to kill, and to destroy. I have come that they may have life, and that they may have it more abundantly. John 10:10*

Abundant life is not found in a bottle, or a needle or a roach clip or in any other thing that man has devised. Satan tempts us with his offering of satisfaction through manmade devices like drugs, alcohol and pornography. He does not tempt us in order to give us a good time, but to kill us, steal from us and ultimately to destroy us. Compare his offer with the one Jesus brings. Instead of destruction and death, Jesus offers real life. He says that your life in Him will super abound. Praise God for the difference! That is one reason why you should be interested in knowing Him more.

Here is another reason why you should want to know God better. Remember that the people of Thessalonica were commended because they had turned to God from idols to serve the living and true God (I Thessalonians 1:9). Notice the order; they turned to God first. You cannot turn from idols without turning to something else. Most of the world's teaching about addictions would have you turn to anything other than your current addiction. That is not what the Bible teaches, and it isn't what will give you abundant life. Turn to Jesus Christ; focus your life on Him, and He will empower you to give up the idolatrous practices in your life.

We have been given the great privilege of getting to know God. Our earliest ancestors – Adam and Eve, had the pleasure of walking with Him in the Garden of Eden. God created them to worship Him and to fellowship with Him. Their sin separated them from God and made it impossible for us to continue in this intimate relationship with God. The separation created a vacuum in our souls that cannot be filled with anything but God. Thank God that He already had a plan – the relationship would be restored through the sacrificial death and resurrection of Jesus Christ. Through Christ, we are united in relationship with God to worship Him and to fellowship with Him. If you don't know God, then you are missing the reason that you were created. Man cannot live a truly fulfilled life without knowing God.

The topic of getting to know God cannot be contained in a single chapter of this book. However, it is contained in one book; it's called the Bible. A lot of our preconceived notions about God are based upon tradition, hearsay or the opinions of other people. It is extremely important to return to God's Word to have your understanding of God rooted in His description of Himself. This is His one and only autobiography. In it, God reveals His nature, His character, how He works in the hearts and lives of men, and much, much more.

Psalm 40:7 says, *Behold, I come; in the scroll of the book it is written of me.* According to the tenth chapter of Hebrews, this is a prophecy of Jesus Christ. It means that the entire Bible is about Jesus. Let's look at the Lord in His own Word.

Get to know the One who gives you real life.

God reveals Himself to us by a number of different names in the Bible. This doesn't mean that He is many different gods; each name describes an aspect of His character. You can think of each name as a title for God. He is not just the chief executive officer; He is also chairman of the board, personnel director, chief financial officer, so on and so forth. Let's take a brief look at some of the names or titles that God has in the Bible.

God is the Eternal One, the Great I AM.

In the third chapter of Exodus, God had an interesting conversation with Moses at the burning bush. It was at this place and time that God called Moses to go back to Egypt and deliver His people out of slavery. Moses was a bit skeptical and asked God what he should say when the Israelites asked who sent him.

> *Then Moses said to God, "Indeed, when I come to the children of Israel and say to them, 'The God of your fathers has sent me to you,' and they say to me, 'What is His name?' What shall I say to them?" And God said to Moses, "I AM WHO I AM." And He said, "Thus you shall say to the children of Israel, 'I AM has sent me to you.'"*
> *Exodus 3:13-14*

This raises the question, "I Am who or I Am what?" Over the next few centuries, God would fill in the blank after I Am. Let me explain. God later revealed Himself to the people of Israel by the name of YHWH, which is usually pronounced as "Jehovah." The Hebrew root for "Jehovah" and "I AM" is the same. Both mean "the Eternal One, the Self-existent One, the One who is All." Both the King James and

New King James versions usually translate Jehovah as "LORD." So, when you read LORD you will know that it refers to Jehovah.

By the name of Jehovah God, He communicates His ability to be all that we need. Throughout the Old Testament, God fills in the blank as He shows various aspects of His nature. In Genesis 22:13-14, Abraham needed a sacrifice for the altar. God revealed Himself to Abraham as Jehovah-jireh (THE LORD Will Provide). In other places, He reveals Himself as the God who heals, the God who brings peace, and the God who is present. Here are six aspects of the nature of God revealed in the Old Testament:

> Jehovah-jireh – I AM your provider (Genesis 22:13-14)
> Jehovah-rapha – I AM your healer (Exodus 15:26)
> Jehovah-nissi – I AM your banner (Exodus 17:8-15)
> Jehovah-shalom – I AM your peace (Judges 6:24)
> Jehovah-tsidkenu – I AM your righteousness (Jeremiah 23:6)
> Jehovah-shammah – I AM ever present (Ezekiel 48:35)

In each case, God told His people something about His character as He met their needs and revealed Himself to them. For example, when they were tired of fighting and hiding from the Midianites in Judges 6:24, God revealed Himself to Gideon as Jehovah shalom – the God of peace. In fact, this name literally means "I am your peace." Do you need peace? God can provide it. Just before Jesus was betrayed, He told the disciples,

Peace I leave with you, My peace I give to you; not as the world gives do I give to you. Let not your heart be troubled, neither let it be afraid. John 14:27

Jesus is your peace. Isn't it reassuring to see that the nature of God the Father in the Old Testament is the same nature that Jesus Christ, God the Son, has in the New Testament?

Look at those six I Am statements. Our God is the Great I AM. Others will disappoint us, but God will not. He is our provider, our healer, the banner that we march under, our peace, our righteousness and He is ever-present. This is just a sample of what the Bible says about our Lord.

In Jesus Christ, you have been given a great gift. You have received a relationship with the only One in the universe who is truly whole, who exists apart from anything else – the Great I AM. Through this relationship, He alone makes you whole. If you are feeling incomplete, it may be because you are leaning upon someone or something other than the Lord.

He is God Almighty

God is described as "God Almighty" or *El Shaddai* 48 times in the Old Testament. What does this mean? *El Shaddai* has two meanings: 1) spoiler or oppressor, and 2) strength-giver. At first glance, this looks like a contradiction, but examine the scriptures a little closer. God is the spoiler or oppressor to those who are living apart from Him, who have never submitted their lives to Him, and continue to live in rebellion to His plan for their lives. Romans 8:7 says *that the carnal mind is in opposition to God; for it is not subject to the law of God neither can it be.* This is the condition of natural man; God is *El Shaddai*, the oppressor or spoiler against unbelief and sin.

However, to believers, He is *El Shaddai*, the strength-giver. Psalm 91 gives us a beautiful picture of God Almighty as the strength-giver and protector of those who trust in Him.

> *He who dwells in the secret place of the Most High shall abide under the shadow of the Almighty (Shaddai). I will say of the LORD, "He is my refuge and my fortress; My God, in Him I will trust." Surely He shall deliver you from the snare of the fowler and from the perilous pestilence. He shall cover you with His feathers, and under His wings you shall take refuge; His truth shall be your shield and buckler. Psalm 91:1-4*

Read the entire Psalm and you will see God Almighty not as a spoiler, but as a loving, strong protector for those who love Him and trust Him. The Psalm ends with God saying,

> *Because he has set his love upon Me, therefore I will deliver him; I will set him on high, because he has known My name. He shall call upon Me, and I will answer him; I*

will be with him in trouble; I will deliver him and honor him. With long life I will satisfy him, And show him My salvation. Psalm 91:14-16

What a difference this makes. Can you say this about your relationship with God? As believers who trust in Christ, He is our strength giver, our protector and our salvation.

God is merciful and gracious.

We usually associate the Old Testament with judgment and wrath, and the New Testament with grace and mercy, but God reveals Himself in mercy, even in the Old Testament.

While Moses was on Mt. Sinai with God, the people of Israel got a bit confused and had Aaron make a golden calf for them to worship. After the Israelites had committed the horrible sin of idolatry, Moses and God had a long conversation. In Exodus 33:18 Moses asked God, "Please show me your glory." God responded and said, "I will make all of my goodness pass before you." So when Moses asked to see the glory of Almighty God, He did not respond by showing Moses His wrath or judgment, but by showing Moses His goodness. Keep in mind that this happened after the children of Israel had committed idolatry and adultery at the base of the mountain.

What does this tell us? God is glorified more in His goodness and mercy than in His wrath. Moses asked to see His glory and God responded by showing Moses His goodness. He is glorified in forgiving us for our sin and setting us free too.

The day after his request, Moses had the opportunity to hear of the glory of God.

And the LORD passed before him and proclaimed, "The LORD, the LORD God, merciful and gracious, long-suffering, and abounding in goodness and truth, keeping mercy for thousands, forgiving iniquity and transgression and sin, by no means clearing the guilty, visiting the iniquity of the fathers upon the children and the children's children to the third and the fourth generation." Exodus 34:6-7

When God revealed His name to Moses, He was also revealing His character or His nature. The first thing God wanted him to know was that the all-powerful God is merciful and gracious. He also wanted Moses to know that those who do not accept His mercy will face His judgment.

This scripture in Exodus helps us understand the grace of God as well as the judgment of God. Let's look at the grace and mercy first.

According to this verse, God abounds in goodness and truth and wants to forgive our iniquity or our destructive lifestyles. God says that He forgives lifestyles of addiction and self-abuse. He also forgives our transgression or habitual sins, and our sin (single offences against God). This is good news. It means that God is able to forgive all of our sins, everything that you and I have done even while we were living destructive lifestyles in bondage to alcohol, drugs and sexual sin.

God the Father is merciful and gracious. In John 3:16, it says that God loves you so much that He gave His only begotten Son. The love that God has for you today is the same love that He expressed to Moses. He has always wanted to extend mercy and grace. If you have accepted His offer of salvation through grace, then you receive His mercy.

Romans 5:8 says that God did not wait for you to turn towards Him before He did what was necessary to forgive you.

But God demonstrates His own love toward us, in that
while we were still sinners, Christ died for us. Romans 5:8

God took action before you and I realized that we needed to be forgiven. He is merciful and gracious, long-suffering and abounding in goodness and truth!

What about the judgment mentioned in Exodus 34:7, "*...and that will by no means clear the guilty, visiting the iniquity of the fathers upon the children, and upon the children's children, unto the third and fourth generation.*"

What does this mean? It is a statistical fact that children of drug addicts are more prone to become drug addicts, that those addicted to alcohol are more likely to have children who are also alcoholics, and that children who are abused by their parents are likely to become parents who abuse their children. The natural outcome of continuing to dwell in sin is for the iniquity or the destructive lifestyles of the fathers to pass from generation to generation. It has been this way since the sin nature of Adam was passed on to his children.

How can this curse be broken? We will use scripture to interpret scripture. In the book of Deuteronomy, God provides some additional understanding to this verse:

You shall not bow down to them nor serve them (idols). For I, the LORD your God, am a jealous God, visiting the iniquity of the fathers upon the children to the third and fourth generations of those who hate Me. Deuteronomy 5:9

So, iniquity is visited upon *those who hate God* to the third and fourth generation. According to the verse in Deuteronomy, we stop the train of iniquity and judgment by *not* hating God. You stopped being a God-hater when you admitted that you were a sinner in need of repentance and received Jesus Christ as Lord and Savior. At that point, you and I were forgiven of ALL sin.

According to I John 1:7 & 9, it is on the basis of His blood and our confession of sin that our sins are forgiven, *"He is faithful and just to forgive us our sins and to cleanse us from all unrighteousness"*.

As a believer in Jesus Christ, you are no longer an enemy of God. You have been washed clean from your sins by the blood of Jesus and you are no longer guilty. He has separated your sins from you as far as the east is from the west. God Almighty is now your strength-giver rather than your spoiler and oppressor. As you focus on Jesus, worship Him and follow Him, He empowers you to stop your abusive, addictive behavior and to break the habits of sin that your fathers lived in if they did not know Jesus. The curse is broken.

On the other hand, if you have not repented of your sin based upon the shed blood of Jesus then you are still in your sin and you stand as an enemy of God (Ephesians 2:15-16, Romans 8:7).

So your decision of whether or not to commit your life to Christ affects a lot of other lives in addition to your own. By admitting your need for Jesus to forgive your sins, you open the door to your children to live new lives in Christ. By your example, they will see the life of Christ in you, and they will see the joy of living as a follower of Jesus rather than living in bondage to sin and addiction.

We see the glory of God revealed in Jesus Christ.

> *For it is the God who commanded light to shine out of darkness, who has shone in our hearts to give the light of the knowledge of the glory of God in the face of Jesus Christ. II Corinthians 4:6*

We see the glory of God in the face of Jesus Christ. On the night that He would be betrayed, Jesus told Phillip,

> *Have I been with you so long, and yet you have not known Me, Philip? He who has seen Me has seen the Father; so how can you say, 'Show us the Father'? John 14:9*

We know God the Father through the revelation of Jesus Christ, His only Son.

Jesus revealed the glory of God and His claim to be God through a series of statements in the gospel of John. Remember that "I AM" and "Jehovah" mean the same thing. The name of Jesus has an interesting connection to these two expressions for God. The Greek name "Jesus" comes from the Hebrew "Joshua," which means "Jehovah is Salvation." Since Jehovah and I AM have the same meaning, the name Jesus literally means "I AM Salvation."

In the eighth chapter of John, Jesus tells the Pharisees exactly who he is. While at the Temple during the Feast of Tabernacles, Jesus engaged these men in a long conversation about His identity. In John 8:58, He concluded by saying, "*Most assuredly, I say to you, before Abraham was, I AM!*" They responded by trying to stone Jesus to death because He was claiming to be equal with God, the Great I AM of the Old Testament.

Throughout the book of John, Jesus makes seven of His own "I AM" statements. Each one reveals more of His nature to you. Here are all seven:

I am the bread of life – John 6:48.
I am the light of the world – John 8:12
I am the door – John 10:9
I am the good shepherd – John 10:11
I am the resurrection and the life – John 11:25

I am the way, the truth and the life – John 14:6
I am the true vine – John 15:1

Jesus and the Great I AM are one. He is the spiritual bread that sustains you and me. He is only source of light in a dark world. He is the door through which you enter eternal life. He is the good shepherd who loves and leads His sheep. He is the source of life brought out of death. In Jesus alone you find the way to salvation, truth and real life. Jesus is the true vine, and you abide in Him as a branch.

I encourage you to read these seven passages in the gospel of John to learn more about the nature of Jesus and to see for yourself that He is who He claims to be. In His claims, Jesus is telling you, "I AM all that you need."

Jesus is meek and lowly of heart.

In a rare autobiographical statement in Matthew, Jesus says volumes about His nature when He invites us to follow Him.

> *Come unto me all ye that labor and are heavy laden, and I will give you rest. Take my yoke upon you and learn of me; for I am meek and lowly in heart, and ye shall find rest for your souls. For my yoke is easy and my burden is light. Matthew 11:28-30*

What does this mean to someone who has struggled with addiction? Let's look at a few key points.

"Labor" in this passage literally means "labor of the soul." Jesus is inviting all who are discouraged, all who are in despair, who are frustrated or living in sorrow to lay down their heartaches and receive rest for their souls.

You may have lived under the burdens of discouragement, depression, frustration and sorrow. You may have tried to lift these burdens on your own through pills, booze or relationships with other people. You were searching for some place of rest and peace. Jesus understands. In this scripture passage, He is telling you that He can remove the burden. Come to Him and He will give you rest.

What does it mean when Jesus says that He is meek and lowly of heart? He is not proud and boastful. He is very approachable. So you can bring Him your problems. You can unload your burdens on Him, and He will give you rest for your soul. Isn't that one of your deepest needs?

Jesus' description of Himself in Matthew opens a door of hope for people who have struggled with addiction. Many have been told that they cannot come to Jesus until they get cleaned up, or they have been told that Jesus alone is not enough to remove the burden of addictive thinking, discouragement, guilt and despair. That is not true. Jesus invites you to come to Him in whatever state you may be in. While He was walking the earth, Jesus was accused of eating with sinners, touching lepers and forgiving prostitutes. He still reaches out to those that the world condemns, to those who may not feel that they are worthy to be forgiven.

Jesus also promises an easy yoke and a light burden. The yoke referred to in Matthew 11:30 was the wooden device that fit over the shoulders of oxen. It was connected by ropes to a cart or plow and enabled the oxen to pull it. The better the yoke fit, the easier it was to pull the weight. Jesus tells us that His yoke is easy. In other words, it is a perfect fit. Our burden is light because He is yoked with us. If you are pulling a heavy burden that is weighing you down, then it is not the one the Lord has designed for you, and you may be pulling it alone. Wouldn't you prefer to serve Jesus rather than laboring under the burden of drug addiction, drunkenness, lust and sexual sin?

You can see more of the heart of Jesus revealed in
Philippians 2: 5-8. This description of His character helps you understand his power, His willingness to forgive your sins, and His desire to give you new life.

> *Let this mind be in you which was also in Christ Jesus, who, being in the form of God, did not consider it robbery to be equal with God, but made Himself of no reputation, taking the form of a bondservant, and coming in the likeness of men. And being found in appearance as a man, He humbled Himself and became obedient to the point of death, even the death of the cross. Philippians 2:5-8*

What do these four short verses tell you about Jesus Christ?
    1. Jesus is the nature of God.

Other Bible verses tell you the same thing. John 1:1 describes Jesus as THE Word who was with God and was God in the beginning of time. John 1:3 says that all things were made by Him. Colossians 1:16-17 says that all things were created by Him and for Him and that by Him all things are held together. Hebrews 1:3 says that Jesus is the express image of the person of God. So you can safely conclude that Jesus is the very nature of God. (Also see Isaiah 9:6, Matthew 1:23, John 17:5, II Corinthians 4:4, Hebrews 1:5, 8.)

    2. He did not think that it was robbery for Him to be equal with God.

Because Jesus is the very form or nature of God, He was not attempting to steal His position of equality with God the Father. You may remember that Lucifer (Satan) tried to steal the glory of God and was cast down from heaven (Isaiah 14:12-17). Jesus is the Creator; Satan is only a created being. There are a number of places in the gospel of John alone where we see Jesus portrayed as equal with God. In John 5:18, the Jews realized that Jesus had made himself equal with God, and they tried to kill Him. In John 5:23, Jesus tells us that those who do not honor the Son do not honor the Father. We have already looked at John 8:58 where Jesus claims to be the Great I AM. In John 10:30 & 33, the Jews accused Jesus of blasphemy again because He said that He is one with the Father.

    3. But Jesus made himself of no reputation.

In other words, He emptied Himself. Jesus, the Son of God, gave away the very thing that most men fight to protect – His reputation. He came to earth as the baby of a poor Hebrew couple and grew up in obedience to His earthly stepfather. He was despised and rejected by men. He came to His own brothers, and they did not receive Him. His humility was prophesied in the Old Testament: Psalm 22:6 – *"I am a worm and no man."* Zechariah 9:9 prophesied that the Messiah would come as lowly, riding on a donkey. This was fulfilled in Matthew 21:1-11. In II Corinthians 8:9, Paul says, *"the grace of our Lord Jesus Christ, that, though he was rich, yet for your sakes he became poor."* Jesus willingly gave up all that was due Him as King of Kings and Lord of Lords when He came to earth as a man.

4. And He took on the form or nature of a bond servant.

Coming down to the level of men was not enough. Jesus placed Himself on the level of a bond servant in order to make it clear that no one was excluded from the kingdom of God on the basis of their position in society. He also modeled for us the most valuable leadership quality in His kingdom - being a servant. In John 13:2-11, Jesus exhibited the example for His disciples to follow when He assumed the job of the lowest house slave and washed their feet. The God we serve was willing to humble Himself to the point of an earthly slave. The same hands that fashioned the universe washed the feet of His disciples, and were later nailed to a cross.

5. And He was made in the likeness (form or resemblance) of men.

In Hebrews 2:14-17, it is explained that as our Great High Priest, it suited Jesus to be made like us in order to be merciful and empathetic. It says, *"In all points He was tempted like us." He was a partaker of flesh and blood that through His death He might destroy him that has power over death, that is the devil* (Hebrews 2:14). Jesus intercedes for you as One who faced temptation and overcame it. In Him, you will overcome temptation too.

6. Jesus humbled himself or allowed Himself to be humiliated.

Jesus did not enjoy the cross. He was humiliated by hanging naked in the place of sinful man. He had the power to come down from the cross, but He stayed for our benefit. He allowed Himself to be humiliated so that we might be glorified together with Him. Hebrews 12:2 explains why He did it. *"Looking unto Jesus the author and finisher of our faith; who for the joy that was set before him endured the cross, despising the shame, and is set down at the right hand of the throne of God."* The Creator of the universe permitted His creation to humiliate Him in order that we might be saved. Proverbs 15:33 reminds us that *"before honor is humility."* Jesus was humiliated; now He receives all of the honor due to Him as the Savior of all men who believe in Him.

7. He became obedient to the point of death, even the death of the cross.

His obedience to the will of the Father extended all the way to death. The Bible says that He became a curse in our place. The willpower we need to overcome sin in our lives is found in Jesus Christ, who had the power to remain obedient to the Father even as He was hanging on the cross outside of Jerusalem. According to Deuteronomy 21:23, those who were hung from a tree were accursed by God, *"his body shall not remain overnight on the tree, but you shall surely bury him that day, so that you do not defile the land which the LORD your God is giving you as an inheritance; for he who is hanged is accursed of God."* This was the greatest insult that a Jewish man could endure. The rabbis believed that such a man was cursed by God, abandoned by both heaven and earth. Being hung on a cross was an ugly, humiliating death.

The curse carried by Jesus to the cross is what enables us to be forgiven of our sins and healed from our iniquities. The power of His blood is the first requirement for a truly free life in Christ. His resurrection from the grave proves that He has power over death and over all that we experience in this life.

There is a lot in these verses that describe our Lord Jesus. He is worthy to be followed, praised and worshipped. Just imagine if one earthly leader was willing to give up his throne or palace or White House to live for 33 years among us, and that he was willing to die as an innocent man, being put to death by the ones he loved. What a powerful story that would be. Jesus did that for you and me.

What does all of this really mean to us? Does knowing Jesus really change our outlook or our circumstances? Jay, a former *Beyond Addictions* student, was serving time in prison when he told me, "Without Jesus in a place like this, there would be no peace. We are never alone; someone is always watching your every move. The other thing is that your mind tends to run loose in here, thinking about everything that is going on outside (of prison). In the midst of all of that, Jesus is my peace."

Another student put it this way, "As I grow closer to Jesus I begin to realize that whatever I looked for in my addiction is provided by Jesus. The closer I get to Him, the more He manifests Himself to me, and allows me to see more and more of His goodness and glory." I would say that the answer is yes, getting to know Jesus radically changes your outlook, and even your circumstances.

Knowing Christ is the real focus of life. The Apostle Paul knew it, gave his whole life to this purpose, and lived one of the most fulfilled lives in history. Many men and women have followed in His footsteps and lived full lives.

In the Christian classic *We Would See Jesus*, author Roy Hession says, "My goal is God Himself, not glory nor power nor even blessing but Himself, my God."[12] He shared the same goal as Paul – to know God better every moment of every day. He wasn't after the gifts that God gives; He was after God Himself. May this be your goal and mine until we see Jesus face-to-face.

There is more to read in the Bible.

There is a great deal about the nature of God in this chapter, but it is just a sample of what the Bible says about the One we worship. Take time to read and meditate on the scriptures that are cited. Read them in your own Bible, underline them and ask the Lord to reveal Himself to you as you study His Word. God has a personality; He has a complete nature. You can trust Him. Read through these verses, and you will see how trustworthy He is. You will see how much He loves you and how strongly He desires for you to be set free from addiction to live a meaningful, fulfilling life in Him.

Here is a little more good news to ponder. God is ...

- Good – Psalm 25:8-10, 33:4-5, I Chronicles 16:34
- Merciful – Psalm 62:12
- Gracious – Psalm 84:11, John 1:14, Ephesians 2:8-9
- Loving – Psalm 63:3, Jeremiah 31:3, Romans 5:8
- Holy – Exodus 15:11, Psalm 22:3, Isaiah 6:3
- Righteous – Psalm 7:9, Daniel 9:7, Ephesians 4:24

---

[12] Roy Hession, *We Would See Jesus*, (England: The Roy Hession Book Trust, 1958), 13.

- Just – Malachi 3:5, Romans 2:11-12, I Peter 1:17
- Wise & Knowledgeable – Job 12:13, Psalm 14, 11:33-36
- True – Deuteronomy 32:4, Psalm 31:5, 86: 15

Got Jesus?

The world offers a lot of solutions to your problems. The Bible provides the real one—Jesus. Think about it. He created you and has a plan for your life, so He probably can provide all you need to fulfill the plan..

It was Jesus who said, "Come unto me all who labor and are heavy laden and I will give you rest." "He whom the Son sets free is free indeed." "I am the bread of life. He who comes to Me shall never hunger, and he who believes in Me shall never thirst."

In chapter 7, you will begin to see that Jesus Christ is sufficient to meet all of your needs, and that you do not need to turn to drugs or alcohol or other addictions to be fulfilled. You are fulfilled in Jesus.

Jesus Christ is Sufficient for All Things

Chapter 7

Knowing that God will supply all of my needs is a great relief to me.
Knowing that He is always with me is a great comfort. He is my
strength, and my protector. Since I came back to Jesus, I no longer have
the desire to use or drink. His grace and mercy is enough for me.
A.H. – *Beyond Addictions* Graduate 2009

Is Jesus really enough? Can you live a fulfilling life trusting only
in the Lord? In the previous chapter we took a glimpse at His nature.
He is truly awesome. The Bible provides an on-going description of
God through a period of more than 4,000 years from the beginning of
Genesis until the final books of the Bible were written near the end of
the first century AD. So the record is there. Let's explore the possibility
that all you and I have needed to live a joyous, fulfilling life has been
waiting for us in Christ.

In *Conformed to His Image*, Kenneth Boa states:

> "People without a relationship with their personal Cre-
> ator are hungering for happiness, meaning and fulfillment
> but nothing this planet offers can fully satisfy these long-
> ings."[13]

Based upon your past experiences and our observations of others,
you probably agree with Dr. Boa. People without faith in God are constantly moving from one thing to another, believing that happiness is
just over the hill or around the next bend. They move from job to job or
house to house searching for fulfillment. They may divorce their spouse
and move in with a neighbor. Some descend deeper and deeper into
drug addiction or alcoholism. Nothing satisfies them for very long.

Where can we find satisfaction and fulfillment?

Let's go back to Samaria where Jesus visited with the woman at
the well. She had tried it all, five husbands and at least one man whom

---

[13] Kenneth Boa, *Conformed to His Image*, (Grand Rapids: Zondervan, 2001).

she wasn't married to. The Bible is silent regarding any other solutions she sought to be fulfilled, but you can imagine that there were others. She finally found all that she ever needed in Jesus Christ. Imagine how her life changed after meeting Jesus at the well. Most likely, she moved away from the man she had been living with. She had a sense of peace and fulfillment so that she no longer needed to lean on physical relationships with men to be satisfied; she was leaning on her Savior. He was all that she needed.

Author John Piper says, "I know of no other way to triumph over sin long-term than to gain a distaste for it because of a superior satisfaction in God." That is how you triumph over sin and remove issues of addiction from your life. As you draw nearer and nearer to Jesus, you realize that you have something far superior to anything that sin can offer. Your own experiences teach you that none of these sinful alternatives work and all of them have some seriously bad side effects like physical illness, financial ruin, loss of family, or prison. When you truly encounter Jesus, like the woman at the well, you find peace. You are filled to overflowing, and you bring others to Him too.

So as a Christian, you have the ability to live an abundant life in Christ. His death on the cross took away your sin. Then He sent another comforter, the Holy Spirit, to counsel you and to guide you day-to-day. John 14:17 says that the Holy Spirit doesn't just come alongside to guide you, He dwells in you. So you no longer need to go out drinkin' and druggin' in order to be fulfilled. You have real life through Jesus Christ.

What does it mean when we say that Jesus is sufficient for all of our needs? 1) He has the complete supply of all that we need to be fulfilled, and 2) He has the desire and ability to provide all that we need. Is this true? What does the Bible say about it?

All things were created by and for Jesus Christ.

For by Him (Jesus) all things were created that are in heaven and that are on earth, visible and invisible, whether thrones or dominions or principalities or powers. All things were created through Him and for Him. Colossians 1:16

Jesus was the creator and all things were made by Him and for Him. You are one of the "all things" that were made by Jesus Christ for Jesus Christ.

A common problem among men is that we are confused regarding the purpose for our lives. The majority of people, including Christians, seem to believe that they are here for their own pleasure and that God is here to help them achieve their goals. Colossians 1:16 says that we were not created for our purposes or pleasure; we were made by Jesus for Jesus. You will never be truly at peace until you understand the purpose for your life. You were created for Jesus. Revelation 4:11 reads this way in the King James Version:

> *Thou art worthy, O Lord, to receive glory and honor and power: for thou hast created all things, and for thy pleasure they are and were created.*

You were created for God's purposes and His pleasure. You cannot live a fulfilling life apart from God or apart from His purpose for you. If you are still wrestling with God for control of the steering wheel, then you cannot live in harmony with Him and you will be frustrated in your relationship with Him. He wants you to enjoy a fulfilling, joyous life; let Him take the wheel and enjoy the trip.

All fullness is found in Christ.
Jesus doesn't just supply the resource we need; He *is* the resource.

> *For it pleased the Father that in him (Jesus), should all fullness dwell. Colossians 1:19*

The Greek word translated "fullness" is *pleroma*. It means "that which fills up, copiousness, multitude." It can be translated "all that is in all." Right now, if you could have the mind of God, the peace of God, the provision of God, what would you lack? Nothing. Guess what? You've have the mind of Christ through your relationship with Jesus. There is nothing about God the Father that is not contained in His Son. He is the exact image of the invisible God. You have constant access to God the Father through Jesus Christ, His Son.

The passage in Colossians 2:3-10 opens a storehouse of treasure that you have in Jesus. Let's look at it.

> *(Christ) in whom are hidden all the treasures of wisdom and knowledge. Now this I say lest anyone should deceive you with persuasive words. Colossians 2:3-4*

All of the wisdom and knowledge that you need for Godly living is found in Christ. If you need advice on how to raise your children, you will find it in Jesus. If you need counsel on how to be a better husband or wife, Jesus has the answers. You may want to excel in your work or to be a better provider. He can tell you how to do it. Have you struggled with frustration or anger? Jesus can give you victory over these problems.

A lot of persuasive words have been written to discourage you from seeking fulfillment in Jesus; however, you don't have to review the pop psychology of every new self-help book to find true wisdom and knowledge. Colossians 2:4 says that you can find it in Jesus. The divinely inspired, time-tested Word of God reveals Christ to you.

> *As you have therefore received Christ Jesus the Lord, so walk in Him, rooted and built up in Him and established in the faith, as you have been taught, abounding in it with thanksgiving. Colossians 2:6-7*

This is important counsel for Christians. Paul tells us that receiving Christ Jesus the Lord is just the beginning. Do you know anyone who prayed to receive Jesus Christ but has not grown closer in their relationship with Him? Unfortunately, this describes many people who had a one-time encounter with Jesus but have not been discipled. They have not grown much, and they probably have not achieved victory over sin.

New life in Christ is just the beginning. Paul tells us to walk in Him, to get rooted in Him and to build up from there. You need to fully establish your life in Christ. Put down roots. Build each day upon what He taught you the day before. Become more and more established in your faith in Jesus. Read the Bible. Get involved in a Bible-teaching church where people share the love of Jesus and worship Him. Pray. Grow.

*Beware lest anyone cheat you through philosc
empty deceit, according to the tradition of men, a
to the basic principles of the world, and not acc
Christ. Colossians 2:8*

Beware. There are many who will tell you that Jesus isn't enough, that you have to add godless philosophies to your faith in Jesus. Paul calls this "empty deceit." He says that the purveyors of this false teaching are attempting to cheat you out of the fullness that Jesus offers you in Him and Him alone.

We live in a time when there is a worldly explanation and a medical diagnosis for everything, and there are pills to treat every problem. Certainly, some of these problems require medical attention; however, in many cases, the real problem is that we have not submitted our lives to Christ. The world's explanations and medications are, in most instances, only temporary treatments. They are band-aids over sores that need to be healed. True healing comes through the fullness that is in Jesus.

For in Him dwells all the fullness of the Godhead bodily, and you are complete in Him, who is the head of all principality and power. Colossians 2:9-10

Memorize these two verses. All of the fullness of God dwells in Jesus Christ, and you are complete in Him. The Greek word translated "complete" also means "fulfilled, satisfied, furnished." It is the same word translated as "full" in John 15:11 where Jesus says, *"These things have I spoken unto you, that my joy might remain in you, and that your joy might be full."* Jesus makes you complete; He offers fullness of joy so that there is nothing lacking. Oh how I need His fullness everyday!

Jesus Christ is sufficient to fulfill you, to counsel you, to give you abundant life, to restore your peace, to provide for you ... the list is as endless as the supply.

Take a note: You do not add anything to your life in Christ Jesus by indulging in sinful addictions. You do not add anything to the fullness of Jesus by pursuing the pleasures of this world. He has it all and you are complete in Him. So rather than looking for the next thrill or chasing the latest promise for real happiness, you can find real joy and real fulfillment in Christ.

God is your provider.

> *The LORD is my shepherd; I shall not want. He makes me to lie down in green pastures; He leads me beside the still waters. He restores my soul; He leads me in the paths of righteousness For His name's sake. Psalm 23:1-3*

This is serious scripture. Can you say this about the shepherd you are following? If not, then you might be following the wrong one. The twenty-third Psalm attributes to God the ability and desire to supply your needs, give you rest, gently lead you, restore your soul and lead you in the paths of right living. These three verses are filled with promises from our Lord. In particular, they say that our Good Shepherd will supply your needs.

The Hebrew word translated "want" in verse one can also be translated "crave." When you follow the Good Shepherd, you are freed from your cravings. Say this out loud, "The LORD is my shepherd, I will not crave."

In Philippians 4:19, the Apostle Paul says, *"My God shall supply all of my needs according to His riches in glory by Christ Jesus."* Paul had learned to turn to Jesus to have his needs met. He didn't go first to the government, to unbelievers, or even to other Christians. He turned to Christ. God may use others as instruments to provide, but the supply comes from Him.

We have personally experienced this thousands of times in our family. We have brought our needs to the throne of God for everything from food to housing to expenses for college to wisdom for how to raise our kids to everything else. As we have waited on the Lord, He has met every need. In the process, He has also helped me separate my needs from my wants, and I have been freed from desiring everything that the world tells me that I should have.

There is no reason to give this task to anyone else who is less able to do the job. Take your needs in prayer to God. You will find that He supplies all of them according to His riches in glory by Christ Jesus.

He is your healer and deliverer.

> *"The Spirit of the LORD is upon Me, Because He has anointed Me to preach the gospel to the poor; He has sent Me to heal the brokenhearted, to proclaim liberty to the captives and recovery of sight to the blind, to set at liberty those who are oppressed; to proclaim the acceptable year of the LORD." Then He closed the book, and gave it back to the attendant and sat down. And the eyes of all who were in the synagogue were fixed on Him. And He began to say to them, "Today this Scripture is fulfilled in your hearing."*
> *Luke 4:18-21*

In this passage, Jesus was speaking of Himself. Compare His offer for healing, deliverance and freedom to the alternatives that you have already tried. Alcohol will not cure a broken heart. Neither will another short-term relationship. This passage in Luke says that Jesus can heal your broken heart. He can also deliver you from the addictive behavior that holds you captive; He can restore your sight and set you free. Jesus can heal you and deliver you from sinful addictions. Now that is GOOD NEWS.

Addiction holds you in darkness. You are constantly living in shadows and hiding your true self from others. You live in fear. Jesus has power to deliver you from darkness.

> *He (God) has delivered us from the power of darkness and conveyed us into the kingdom of the Son of His love:*
> *Colossians 1:13*

God has already delivered you from the power of darkness. A lot of folks are still looking for deliverance. He has already accomplished it. It's time to walk in the deliverance that He has provided.

He satisfies your thirst.

Some addictions continue because the addictive substance or activity partially satisfied a thirst or a craving. The satisfaction was very temporary. You had to go back every day for a fresh hit or a drink. Then you had to have it twice a day and later you sought it more often. In between, you were anxious, paranoid, fearful, and empty. The sorry wells of addiction kept you coming back for more of the same bitter water. When you come to the wellspring of Jesus He fills you with refreshing, cleansing, living water. And you will not struggle with the fear and guilt, or anxiety and emptiness.

> *Whoever drinks of this water will thirst again but whoever drinks of the water that I shall give him will never thirst. But the water that I shall give him will become in him a fountain of water springing up into everlasting life. John 4:13-14*

Jesus doesn't give you a "sugar high" that last for a short time. He satisfies your thirst in such a way that you know that you will never be satisfied drinking from any other well.

He has given you and me all things that pertain to life.

> *Grace and peace be multiplied to you in the knowledge of God and of Jesus our Lord, as His divine power has given to us all things that pertain to life and godliness, through the knowledge of Him who called us by glory and virtue. II Peter 1:2-3*

Again, the Bible teaches that all wisdom and knowledge is found in Christ. All things that pertain to real life can be found in knowing Jesus. Looking anywhere other than Christ is simply a distraction and a waste of time. Peter says that God has given these things to you through the knowledge of Jesus. The closer you are to the Lord, the more you receive the knowledge and wisdom necessary for life and godliness. The divine power needed to obtain these things is provided by the Holy Spirit and the knowledge of Jesus is found by reading and meditating on His Word.

He counsels you.

I know that we have already addressed this topic, but some of it bears repeating. Jesus is our Wonderful Counselor.

> *For unto us a Child is born, Unto us a Son is given; And the government will be upon His shoulder. And His*

name will be called Wonderful, Counselor, Mighty God, Everlasting Father, Prince of Peace. Isaiah 9:6

This prophecy of Jesus calls Him, among other names, our Wonderful Counselor. We can and we should go to Jesus in prayer before seeking counsel from other men or women.

> *I will instruct you and teach you in the way you should go; I will guide you with My eye. Do not be like the horse or like the mule, which have no understanding, which must be harnessed with bit and bridle, else they will not come near you. Psalm 32:8-9*

In Psalm 32, God promises to counsel you with His eye. This is a close relationship between the one directing and the one receiving the direction. He looks and you know what He means. In order to be guided by His eye you need to be looking at Him.

In comparison, He warns us not to be like a stubborn mule that requires a bit and bridle in order to be controlled. How many times did God draw you before you answered? Now that you know Him, submit your life to Him. Keep your eye on Him and follow His direction.

Warning: as you walk the road with Jesus, do not be fooled by anyone who seems to offer you a better deal. Paul had this concern for the believers in Corinth and it goes for us too:

> *But I fear, lest somehow, as the serpent deceived Eve by his craftiness, so your minds may be corrupted from the simplicity that is in Christ. II Corinthians 11:3*

He was concerned that the Christians in Corinth would be turned aside from the simplicity of trusting Jesus by those who seemed to offer something that was more effective. There have always been charlatans who have tried to draw people away from the simplicity of trusting Jesus. Some want to control you, others want your money, some just want you to buy their books or DVDs. Just keep your focus on Jesus. Isaiah 26:3 contains a wonderful promise for those who keep their minds on Christ:

You (God) will keep him in perfect peace, whose mind
is stayed on You, because he trusts in You. Isaiah 26:3

Do you see the harmony between Paul's concern in II Corinthians and the promise in Isaiah? The verse in Isaiah promises peace to those who simply trust God. You will be at peace if you trust in the simplicity of Jesus Christ. Keep your mind focused on Him.

Your sufficiency is not in yourself; it is in Christ.

By now, you probably realize that Jesus Christ is sufficient; He is enough. In fact, He is all that you need. There is one more point that needs to be covered. You may be tempted to believe that you were fairly sufficient before you met Jesus and that you just needed a little help from Him to finish the job. Paul corrects this misconception in his second letter to the Corinthian church:

> *For we do not want you to be ignorant, brethren, of our trouble which came to us in Asia: that we were burdened beyond measure, above strength, so that we despaired even of life. Yes, we had the sentence of death in ourselves, that we should not trust in ourselves but in God who raises the dead, who delivered us from so great a death, and does deliver us; in whom we trust that He will still deliver us. II Corinthians 1:8-10*

Many Bible scholars believe that this event occurred in Lystra during Paul's first missionary journey when he was stoned and dragged out of town. Paul says that this situation pressed him beyond the measure of his own strength so that he lost hope in living. Have you ever been in such a situation? You may not have faced the trial of a threatened death sentence, but you have faced a great deal of discouragement over circumstances in your life. Why did God permit this to happen? According to Paul it was so *"that we should not trust in ourselves but in God who raises the dead who delivered us from so great a death and does deliver us in whom we trust that He will still deliver us!"*

God allowed Paul to reach a point beyond his ability to deliver himself. He could not save himself by physical strength or his brilliant mental abilities or his powers of persuasion. All that Paul could do was trust Jesus. Jesus' great deliverance increased Paul's faith so that he knew Jesus could deliver him out of any situation he found himself in as a servant of God.

You can probably relate to Paul. Addiction eventually took you to the point of hopelessness, of being burdened beyond measure so that you despaired even of life. You saw no way out of the pit. The correct response when you reached this point was not to trust in your own abilities but in God who raises the dead. He has delivered you from death in sin and continues to deliver. You can trust that He will deliver you daily from the sin that hindered you in the past.

> *And we have such trust through Christ toward God. Not that we are sufficient of ourselves to think of anything as being from ourselves, but our sufficiency is from God. II Corinthians 3:4-5*

We don't bring anything to the party. If you have felt that you didn't have much to offer God, then rejoice. He has all that you need, and He did not expect you to bring anything of your own into His kingdom. Your sufficiency is from God. Amen! Amen! Amen!

In John 15:5, Jesus teaches us how much you or I or anyone else can do apart from Him.

> *I am the vine, you are the branches. He who abides in Me, and I in him, bears much fruit; for without Me you can do nothing. John 15:5*

If you abide in Jesus, then you will enjoy a fruitful life, but apart from Jesus you can do nothing. Philippians 4:13 takes the power of Jesus Christ a bit further when it says, *"I can do all things through Christ, who strengthens me."* "All things" includes defeating addictions and breaking down strongholds. Without Jesus you can do nothing; in Christ Jesus you can do all things; you can leave the bondage to sin behind and walk freely into the future.

So, all sufficiency is in Jesus Christ, and none of it is in us. When people see the change that Jesus has made in your life and mine, God is glorified, and they know where to go to have their lives changed too. This is the message of II Corinthians 4:6-7:

For it is the God who commanded light to shine out of darkness, who has shone in our hearts to give the light of the knowledge of the glory of God in the face of Jesus Christ. But we have this treasure in earthen vessels, that the excellence of the power may be of God and not of us.
II Corinthians 4:6-7

Our failures can come to an end. You and I were not made to part ways with addictions or other sinful habits on our own. Instead, we can bring our problems and trials and pain to Jesus and invite Him to shoulder the burden. He will relieve you of the load, and He will be glorified in the process.

Over and over again, scripture teaches the great news that our sufficiency should not be and cannot be of ourselves. Our sufficiency is in Christ! Now you see why it has been impossible for you to live an abundant life without Jesus. He alone is sufficient, and He loves you completely. He has a good plan for your life.

In this chapter, you have learned that your sufficiency in Christ can break you free from the bondage of addiction because. . . .

- He is the Creator and all things were made for Him.
- All fullness is found in Christ.
- He is my provider.
- He is my healer and deliverer.
- He satisfies my thirst.
- He has given me all things that pertain to life.
- He counsels me.
- I don't bring anything to the party; my sufficiency is in Christ.

Foundational scripture ...

According as His divine power has given to us all things that pertain to life and godliness, through the knowledge of Him who called us by glory and virtue. II Peter 1:3

The thief does not come except to steal, and to kill, and to destroy. I have come that they may have life, and that they may have it more abundantly. John 10:10

For I know the thoughts that I think toward you, says the LORD, thoughts of peace and not of evil, to give you a future and a hope. Jeremiah 29:11

For the eyes of the LORD run to and fro throughout the whole earth, to show Himself strong on behalf of those whose heart is loyal to Him. II Chronicles 16:9a

Who are you?

This world is filled with people who do not know who they are. Some attempt to find their identity in gangs, or by climbing the social ladder.

You have probably heard of people reaching mid-life and having an identity crisis. They realize that the things they have valued most have little real meaning, and they reject it all to go "find themselves."

A life of purpose is rooted in knowing who you are. Jesus holds the key to finding your true identity. He told us that the only way to really find our life is to lose it in Him. This is how one graduate of the first Beyond Addictions course sums it up.

We all want to live the "good life" to have real peace and happiness, to be free from addiction. If you have ever been addicted to anything, you tend to go through life thinking that if I could just stop the addictive behavior, all would be fine. I assure you that it wouldn't be! We simply move from worshipping the addiction to worshipping not using or participating in that lifestyle, and we remain in bondage. Any effort to quit in your own power is typically short lived or places you in bondage to not using, and never frees you to worship Christ.

In 2002 I participated in the first Beyond Addictions class, which was and continues to be an integral part of my life and faith in Christ. This class helped me understand who I was in Christ, which transitioned me from a user of drugs and people to a worshipper of Jesus Christ. As I began to know who I was in Christ, the desire to worship Him grew, and the old lifestyle simply began to fall away. I encourage you to not just read but put into practice the contents of this book and you'll find that in worshipping Jesus, you'll truly find the "good life."

Jeremy Parker, *Beyond Addictions* Graduate 2002

Your New Identity in Christ

Chapter 8

Jesus Christ gave his life for you
so that he could give his life to you
so that he could live his life through you.
Kenneth Boa, *Conformed to His Image*

In chapter six, you learned a bit about the loving and forgiving nature of Jesus Christ. In chapter seven, you learned that Jesus is sufficient for all of your needs. Get ready for another amazing message that the Bible has for you as a believer in Jesus Christ. God wants you to know what He thinks of you and who you really are as His child.

In times past, you were identified by your old nature and your old behavior (drunkard, dope head, womanizer) or by your family ("Stay away from him; his family never did amount to much."). Or you may have been known by your performance in school (bright but lazy, he talks all of the time).

I have some good news. When you accepted Jesus Christ as your Lord and Savior, you were given a new nature, a new identity. You are now a truly new person. Speaking of you and me, the Apostle Paul says,

> *Therefore, if anyone is in Christ, he is a new creation; old things have passed away; behold, all things have become new. II Corinthians 5:17*

You are a new creation, and God now identifies you according to your new, spiritual nature. How can this be? First of all, this isn't a matter of you coming to Jesus and beginning to behave differently. It isn't a matter of trying harder to be good just because you appreciate what Jesus has done for you. It is a matter of Jesus Christ making you new by the power of His blood and the work of the Holy Spirit.

Does your behavior change? Yes. But the change in your behavior is caused by the change in your nature.

Pastor A.W. Tozer put it this way:

> Sometimes Evangelical Christians seem to be fuzzy and uncertain about the nature of God and His purposes in creation and redemption. In such instances, the preachers often are to blame. There are still preachers and teachers who say that Christ died so we would not drink and not smoke and go to the theater. No wonder people are confused! No wonder they fall into the habit of backsliding when such things are held up as the reason for salvation.
>
> Jesus was born of a virgin, suffered under Pontius Pilate, died on the cross and rose from the grave to make worshippers out of rebels![14]

In other words, Jesus did not come just to get you to break sinful habits. The result of His coming was greater than that, and the effect that He has on your life is deeper than that. When you accepted Jesus, He changed your nature and your identity. Once a rebel, you are now a worshipper of Jesus Christ. As we worship the Lord and grow closer to Him, we part ways with our old sinful nature.

Old things are passed away. Jesus put away your old nature when He took away your sin at the cross. According to I John 1:7, as a believer in Jesus Christ, the blood of Jesus cleanses you from all sin. In fact, God no longer associates your sin with you anymore:

> *As far as the east is from the west, so far hath he removed our transgressions from us. Psalm 103:12*

In the eyes of Christ, you are no longer a drug addict or a drunk or an adulterer. The blood of Jesus removed that sin from you. As a new creation in Christ, you are empowered by the Holy Spirit to live a new life with a new spiritual nature. So you can stop dragging the baggage from the past around with you.

---

[14] A.W. Tozer, *Whatever Happened to Worship*, (Camp Hill: Christian Publications, 1985), 11.

All things become new. In John 1:42, Jesus changed Simon's name to Cephas (or Peter). Cephas means "a stone." So, this man who was as unstable as water before he met Jesus became a stone in the foundation of the church because of his new relationship with Jesus. The grace of our Lord is so great that He can do this in the life of everyone who trusts in Him.

We mentioned Nicodemus earlier. He came to Jesus to find out how anyone could enter the kingdom of God. Jesus told him, *"Unless one is born again he cannot see the kingdom of God"* (John 3:3). Nicodemus was a well-educated man who believed that he lived according to the holiness of the law. Jesus was telling him that his position in the kingdom of God would not be earned by his education or by any personal holiness that he assumed to have. Our ability to enter the kingdom of God is not based upon our works or education or personal holiness either. It is based upon faith in the blood of Jesus and being born again of the Holy Spirit.

In Luke 18:18, a certain ruler asked Jesus what he had to do to inherit eternal life. He was looking at the issue from the wrong angle. The issue isn't what you can do; the issue is who you are in Jesus. If you have a relationship with Jesus based upon His shed blood for the forgiveness of your sin, then you have eternal life and the Spirit of God dwells in you. This changes who you are. In Tozer's words, you stop being a rebel and you become a worshipper of Jesus. You are given a new, spiritual nature.

Many Bible teachers make the same mistake as the ruler in Luke 18. They focus on what God wants you to do without taking time to see who God wants you to be. He wants you to be His child, born not of the will of the flesh or of the will of man, but of God (John 1:12-13). Once you are born again as a believer in Jesus, and you begin to understand what He says about who you are as His child, then you start to do things that please Him. As Kenneth Boa says, "'Being' always precedes 'Doing' and 'Doing' can only flow out of our 'Being.'"[15]

I'll use my own family as an example. My wife and I love our children. They have a secure place in our family, not because of what they do to please us, but because they are our children. They didn't earn this right; they were given to us by God. They are my sons and daugh-

---

[15] Kenneth Boa, *Conformed to His Image*, (Grand Rapids: Zondervan, 2001).

ters. This sense of who they are as members of our family also influences how they behave. Their desire to please their parents is rooted in the love that we have for them, and that they have for us.

In the same way, our identity as sons and daughters in the family of God influences our behavior. Who we *are* as Christians effects what we *do* as Christians. As Mr. Boa puts it, our "being" as His children determines our "doing."

Think about who you are as a believer in Jesus Christ, as a child of the living God, and let's take a look at what the Bible says about your new identity in Christ.

You have been chosen by God.

Have you ever wanted to be chosen for a special assignment? Well, you have been.

> *Blessed be the God and Father of our Lord Jesus Christ, who has blessed us with every spiritual blessing in the heavenly places in Christ, just as He chose us in Him before the foundation of the world, that we should be holy and without blame before Him in love, having predestined us to adoption as sons by Jesus Christ to Himself, according to the good pleasure of His will. Ephesians 1:3-5*

Why did God choose you? According to Ephesians 1:3-5, it was to display His love. This passage says a mouthful about God's love for you. Here are just a few points: 1) the God of all creation chose you, 2) so that you could live a life that is separated to Him in love and 3) that all of this was done according to the good pleasure of His will. He loved you and He drew you to Himself. Now you have the privilege of living in His good pleasure.

What else does the Bible say about your selection as a follower of Jesus Christ?

> *But you are a chosen generation, a royal priesthood, a holy nation, His own special people, that you may proclaim the praises of Him who called you out of darkness into His marvelous light. I Peter 2:9*

You are part of a chosen group of people, part of the king's family of priests. The Old Testament priests were responsible for representing God to men, and representing men to God. This is what we do as believer-priests; we are representatives of God to those who are lost. You are also part of a group of people who have been set apart to worship the Lord. You are one of His own special people.

God has adopted you into His family.

Ephesians 1:5 says that you, as a Christian, were adopted into the family of God by Jesus Christ. Welcome to the family! Romans 8:14-15 helps you understand this a little better, and it shows you one of the benefits of being adopted by God.

> *For as many as are led by the Spirit of God, these are sons of God. For you did not receive the spirit of bondage again to fear, but you received the Spirit of adoption by whom we cry out, "Abba, Father." Romans 8:14-15*

By grace, God has adopted you into His family. You were not born into it, and you did not do anything to earn it. He chose you and brought you into His home. As an adopted child of God, you are no longer an orphan of the world or a servant to sin. You have a new identity as a child of our Heavenly Father. You do not have to indulge in the ways of the world just to get by because your Father has promised to supply all of your needs. You no longer have to sell yourself on the street in attempt to find love because your loving Heavenly Father holds you in His perfect, pure embrace.

Years ago some close friends of ours adopted seven Russian orphans. These children had lived in an abusive home and in various orphanages. The life of Russian orphans is extremely hard and unloving, and many of them flee the orphanages because of abuse or harsh treatment. Some choose instead to live on the streets, going down in the sewers to sniff glue and escape the severe winter cold. These seven children had learned how to survive in this brutal environment.

Then amazingly, these children were rescued from the harsh environment of Russian orphans and placed in the care of two loving Christian parents. Within a few days they were given new names and moved to their new home in the United States. Imagine the shock of it all.

They were in a new, permanent home with trees, a yard, and room to play. Best of all, they had loving parents.

Initially, the children weren't accustomed to their new life and they still acted like residents of the orphanage. They took food from the kitchen and hid it in their rooms; they stuffed their clothes under the covers at night so that no one would take them. Their new father and mother continued to love them and to reassure them, "You are our children now. This is your home. Everything in the kitchen is yours; you don't have to hide food in your room." "Put your clothes in the hamper. You can trust that they will be returned to you clean." Whenever the parents disciplined the children, they tried to help them understand that they were loved and that they had a new life in their family. "You are our son and we love you. What you have done is wrong and it isn't what we are about as a family." Over time, the children began to respond to their new parents and they began to accept their new life.

As the children realized that they had a new life and a new identity, their old ways faded away. They were no longer orphans who had to make their own way through the streets; they were sons and daughters of caring parents in a loving home. As they understood their new life and their new identity, their behavior began to change.

Over time, their happiness and success has been in direct relationship to their willingness to discard their old ways and to embrace their new life as children in a loving, stable family.

When God adopted us into His family, we also brought some baggage from our past - old sinful habits that are not part of our new nature. You may still struggle with old sins of lust, anger and pride. If so, you need to let go of the past and receive the love of your heavenly Father. You are in his family now. So, if you are still dabbling in drug use, looking at pornographic pictures or living for other pleasures of this life, then you need to stop. That isn't who you are anymore, and it isn't part of your new life in Christ. There is no need to go back to the streets or into the sewer. God has adopted you into His family. You have a new spiritual nature and a new home with Him in the heavenlies.

You are now redeemed by God to Himself.

In Him we have redemption through His blood, the forgiveness of sins, according to the riches of His grace. Ephesians 1:7

For all have sinned and fall short of the glory of God, being justified freely by His grace through the redemption that is in Christ Jesus. Romans 3:23-24

Redemption means "to deliver by paying a price." You and I had a problem. We were sinners and we owed a debt for our sin that we could not pay. Jesus loves us so much that He intervened and paid our debt in His own blood. Only Jesus could deliver us out of sin, and He has done it. This incredible gift is described in chapter five of the Book of Romans:

But God demonstrates His own love toward us, in that while we were still sinners, Christ died for us. Romans 5:8

Jesus Christ paid the debt for all of our drunkenness, violence, drug use, adultery and other sin. That old debt is no longer hanging over our heads. You and I are debt-free because of the blood of Jesus, and we can live like debt-free men and women.

He has made you alive for the first time.

And you He made alive, who were dead in trespasses and sins. Ephesians 2:1

Even when we were dead in trespasses, made us alive together with Christ (by grace you have been saved), and raised us up together, and made us sit together in the heavenly places in Christ Jesus, that in the ages to come He might show the exceeding riches of His grace in His kindness toward us in Christ Jesus. Ephesians 2:5-7

Most people believe that death means extinction. Death actually means that you are separated from something or someone. You probably have relatives who have gone on to be with the Lord. They are dead to you or separated from you, but they are very much alive to Jesus Christ. There are other people who are physically alive; their heart is beating and their brainwaves are functioning, but they are spiritually dead because they are still separated from God.

The Bible says that we were dead to Christ when we were living in sin. In other words, we were separated from Him because of our sin. As a result, we had no spiritual life, no real joy, no real peace or love. When we were given new life in Christ Jesus, we began to experience real joy, peace and love for the first time.

As a believer in Jesus, God has made you alive to Him and with Him so that you now have real spiritual, eternal life. This is radically different from the old life that we knew. In my experience, it was like walking from a dingy gray existence into a world of living color.

You are His workmanship.

For we are His workmanship, created in Christ Jesus for good works, which God prepared beforehand that we should walk in them. Ephesians 2:10

Based upon your past performance, you may have thought that you were the product of some shoddy workmanship. That is not true anymore. You are now God's workmanship, created in Christ Jesus, and God is at work in your life. In Philippians 1:6, you are assured that He will complete what He has started. There are no unfinished projects in God's workshop.

You are complete in Him.

For in Him dwells all the fullness of the Godhead bodily; and you are complete in Him, who is the head of all principality and power. Colossians 2:9-10

We addressed this in chapter seven, but since it is an important part of your new nature, it bears repeating here. All of the fullness of God dwells in Jesus Christ, and you are complete in Him. This is some of the best news in scripture. You don't need to look for a bottle, or a joint, or some illicit sex to try to be complete or to escape the emptiness you feel. You are complete in Christ. You can come to Him, and He will meet your needs.

... His divine power has given to us all things that pertain to life and godliness, through the knowledge of Him who called us by glory and virtue. II Peter 1:3

The source of your completion is Christ. He gives you all things that are necessary for righteous living. The closer you are to Jesus, the more you receive what is needed for you to live a good, godly life.

The relationship that is most crucial to life is the one that you and I ignored or ran from for years – it is our relationship with Jesus Christ. Before you pick up the phone to call a friend or pick up a book to search for knowledge, sit with the Lord and talk with Him; ask Him to answer your questions. His divine power has made everything available to you that is necessary for godly living, and this incredible resource is found in knowing Jesus Christ.

In *Conformed to His Image*, Kenneth Boa explains your new identity this way:

> Our former identity in Adam was put to death, our new eternal identity in Christ became a living reality when we placed our faith in Him. Without Christ, we were out of harmony with God, life was all about self and we were driven to use people, things and circumstances to meet our needs. In Christ, we are in harmony with God; for us as believers, life should be all about the One who has already fully met our needs.[16]

As you can see, your identity in Jesus Christ is vastly different from the one you had before He entered your life. You are a new creation in Christ Jesus and this changes everything – the way you view the world, the way you work, your ideas about love, your attitude towards people, everything. As you read your Bible and get to know Jesus more, you lose desire for old sinful habits. The old things have passed away; all things have become new.

The following story is told of the early church father Augustine who lived in North Africa from 354-430 AD. He grew up in a good family, but as a young boy he was influenced by bad companions and became a drunkard, a thief and a womanizer.

---

[16] Ibid.

Looking for answers, Augustine studied philosophy, paganism and other world religions. He traveled far from home, working in Carthage, Rome and Milan, but none of his studies or experiences satisfied his longing for real truth.

At 31 years of age while studying in Milan, Augustine came to faith in Jesus Christ. He soon returned to his home in North Africa, and as he was walking down the street one day, a harlot recognized him from years ago. She called out to him, "Augustine!" But he just kept walking. She cried louder, "Augustine, Augustine!" But he paid her no attention. Thinking that he may not have recognized her, she yelled, "Augustine, it's me!" Augustine stopped, turned around and said, "I know, but it's not me." Augustine was no longer the young man who found pleasure in sexual immorality; he was a new creation in Christ Jesus. The woman may have been the same person with the same old nature, but he was not. By living according to his new spiritual nature, Augustine was free from the sins of the past. He had been set free by the same truth that we can apply in Romans 13:13-14:

> *Walk properly, as in the day, not in revelry and drunkenness, not in lewdness and lust, not in strife and envy. But put on the Lord Jesus Christ, and make no provision for the flesh, to fulfill its lusts. Romans 13:13-14*

When Satan uses the old temptations of this world to cry out, "Hey it's me!" you can resist because you are a new person in Christ; you have a new nature and a new identity. You can say to those old temptations, "I know who you are, but it's not me."

Galatians 2:20 sums up the reason that we can live a new life in Jesus.

> *I have been crucified with Christ; it is no longer I who live, but Christ lives in me; and the life which I now live in the flesh I live by faith in the Son of God, who loved me and gave Himself for me. Galatians 2:20*

You have been crucified with Christ. The old nature was put to death. As a new creation, the life of Jesus dwells in you. So you and I live this new life by faith in the Son of God who loved us so much that He gave Himself for each of us. That changes everything!

110

Remember, no more an addict, you are now ...

- Chosen by God
- Adopted in His family
- Redeemed to God
- Alive to Christ
- His workmanship
- Complete!!!

You are a new creation in Jesus Christ. This applies to every area of your life. Is Satan trying to convince you that you are still a drug dealer? Tell him that isn't who you are any more. Does he try to remind you of years of abuse and convince you that you are not worth much? Tell him that you are the king's child and you are much loved.

Take a few minutes and think about the areas in your life where this truth is most needed. Then continue daily to be transformed by the renewal of your mind as you read the Bible and take God at His Word. Read the following scripture passages until you have a clear understanding of your new identity as a believer in Christ.

Who does God say I am?

The following list of scripture passages is taken from *Conformed to His Image* by Kenneth Boa. This is just a sample of what the Bible says about you as a believer in Jesus.

I am a child of God.   John 1:12

I am a branch of the true vine, and a conduit of Christ's life. John 15:1,5

I am a friend of Jesus. John 15:15

I have been justified and redeemed. Romans 3:24

My old self was crucified with Christ, and I am no longer a slave to sin. Romans 6:6

I will not be condemned by God. Romans 8:1

I have been set free from the law of sin and death. Romans 8:2

As a child of God, I am a fellow heir with Christ. Romans 8:17

I have been accepted by Christ. Romans 15:7

I have been called to be a saint. Col. 1:2

In Christ, I have wisdom, righteousness and sanctification. I Cor. 1:30

My body is the temple of the Holy Spirit who dwells in me. I Cor. 3:16

I am a new creature in Christ. II Cor. 5:17

I have become the righteousness of God in Christ. II Cor. 5:21

I have been made one with all who are in Christ. Gal. 3:28

I am no longer a slave but a child and an heir. Gal. 4:7

I have been set free in Christ. Gal. 5:1

I have been blessed with every spiritual blessing in heavenly places. Ephes. 1:3

I am chosen, holy and blameless before God.   Ephes. 1:4

I am redeemed and forgiven by the grace of God. Ephes. 1:7

I have been sealed with the Holy Spirit of promise. Ephes. 1:13

Because of God's mercy and love, I have been made alive with Christ. Ephes. 2:4-5

I am seated in heavenly places with Christ. Ephes. 2:6

I am God's workmanship created to produce good works. Ephes. 2:10

I have been brought near to God by the blood of Christ. Ephes. 2:13

I am a member of God's body and a partaker of His promise. Ephes. 3:6

I have boldness and confident access to God through faith in Christ. Ephes. 3:12

My new self is righteous and holy. Ephes. 4:24

I was formerly darkness, but now am light in the Lord. Ephes. 5:8

I am a citizen of heaven. Phil. 3:20

The peace of God guards my heart and mind. Phil. 4:7

God supplies all my needs. Phil. 4:19

I have been made complete in Christ. Col. 2:10

I have been raised up with Christ. Col. 3:1

My life is hidden with Christ in God. Col. 3:3

Christ is my life, and I will be revealed with Him in glory. Col. 3:4

I have been chosen by God, and I am holy and beloved. Col. 3:12

God loves me and has chosen me. I Thess.1:4

Making the Change

Chapter 9

Obedience flows out of trust.
We either obey the desires of our own hearts
or the Word of the God who made us,
loves us and redeemed us.

Time out

A wise educator once said that a man cannot learn any more than he has time to contemplate, so we are pausing to contemplate what we have studied in the first eight chapters. Take a deep breath and think about what you have covered so far. Together, we have looked at the issue of addiction in scripture. We have also looked at our incredible God, the awesome resources we have in Him, and your new identity as a believer in Jesus Christ. There is a lot to think about.

Pray and ask the Lord to bring the messages of these first eight chapters to life for you. Jesus promised in John 14:26 that the Holy Spirit would lead us into all truth and cause us to remember what He has taught us. So, as we continue to study God's Word, the Holy Spirit is faithful to bring it to our mind when we need it.

Prayerfully ask yourself some questions. The answers will help you determine the strength of your new life's foundation.

1. Am I only seeking a solution to my problems, or am I seeking Jesus?

Do you remember the two thieves on the cross? One wanted Jesus to take him down. The other wanted Jesus to take him up. The first man wanted Jesus to solve his rather severe earthly problem – he was being crucified. He had a very legitimate problem, but he didn't seem at all interested in eternal things; he just wanted Jesus to get him out of the mess that he was in. The second man wanted Jesus. He asked Jesus to remember him when Jesus entered His kingdom. His mind was focused on heavenly things.

It's easy to get caught in the trap of wanting only a solution to your problems. After all, some of your problems are real, and they need to be addressed. Though none may be quite as urgent as relief from crucifixion, they are quite painful and cry out for help.

Thank God that He does solve problems; however, if we are seeking Him only as a problem-solver, then we are not truly worshipping Him. If we are dissatisfied with His methods or His timing, we may be tempted to look for another solution. Then we are likely to find a new idol, a new addiction. I have known people who became discouraged with Jesus and moved in with someone only to find that their new partner was more abusive than their old addiction. I've seen Christians become frustrated with the Lord's timing in fixing their marriage and grow bitter and resentful. They never seem to find the place of peace and contentment that they are seeking.

When we determine to follow Jesus for the sake of following Jesus, then solutions to our problems take their rightful priority. We worship God regardless of whether or not things are going our way. We are also thankful for His deliverance from some issues, and we are thankful for His grace that enables us to endure others.

There is great power in that old gospel song that says, "I have decided to follow Jesus. There's no turning back, no turning back." That is a decision. It is a resolution that says, "Come what may, I am going to follow Jesus. Whether the problems go away or not, I'm going to follow Jesus." Make sure that this is the resolution in your heart. There really is no turning back. Where else would you go?

2. Am I pursuing things that will last (eternal) or things that will pass away (temporal)?

Many people spend their lives chasing dreams for temporary satisfaction. You may meet these people in the supermarket, and they will tell you about their new girlfriend or boyfriend. Six weeks later you will see them in the post office looking glum and beaten down. Then they will tell you that they left their latest true love and that they are searching for another. They are never truly happy.

God wants to move you from a place of seeking temporary satisfaction to the heavenly place of eternal satisfaction. A six-pack of beer provides very temporary help. It gives you a little buzz, but it cannot provide any real peace or joy.

True joy and happiness are not found in an abundance of earthly pleasures or possessions. Have you ever purchased anything that gave you real happiness? How long did the thrill of owning a new car or a new entertainment system last? Real life, real joy and real happiness are not found in what we own, and they aren't found in temporary escapes in bottles, powders, pills or sexual escapades. Real life, peace, joy and happiness are given to us as we seek Jesus. You will not find them anywhere else. Real happiness is a natural result of living in Christ.

3. Am I being shaped by the world or by the Word?

What are you watching on TV? What are you reading? What are you gazing at on the Internet? Are you giving God the best time of the day in prayer and Bible reading? The answers to these questions determine whether you are changing the way you think by renewing your mind.

Watch for the "yea ... buts" in life. It is easy to come to Christ and continue to dabble in sin. As a result, you have no sense of peace and very little real growth. Your conversations with other Christians are filled with "yea ... buts" like, "Yea, I know that I should be growing as a Christian, but I'm just not feeling it." "Yea, I know that I need to stop looking at pornographic pictures, but God knows that it's tough being in prison and He knows my heart."

In many cases, the reason that Christians do not achieve real victory in their lives is because they are continuing to allow their thoughts to be shaped by a sinful world. We have enough sense to close the window if the wind is blowing in the stench from the cesspool. We should also know enough to close the door on the stench that the enemy wants to continue to pour into our minds.

So close the backdoor of your mind to the inputs of this world, open the front door, and receive the fresh air that God brings through His Word. Then you will experience more victory over sin.

4. What do my priorities reveal about me?

You can tell a lot about a person by their daily schedule and their checkbook. Where are you investing your time and your money? The answers to these questions will reveal whether you are a doer of God's Word or just a hearer.

Remember, if you are just a hearer, then it is easy to become self-deceived. Again, it is easy to spend five minutes with God in the morning, say a little prayer as you are going out the door and believe that you have allowed Him to direct your day. Than later, you may cop an attitude towards Him because you are experiencing some problems or because He doesn't seem to be answering your prayers.

Take another approach. Spend some real time with the Lord. Invest yourself in knowing Him and in understanding the Bible. Allow God to direct your priorities. Jot down what you believe your highest priorities to be. Then pray over this short list and ask the Holy Spirit to organize your day according to these priorities. Follow His lead. You will be blessed as you do.

This will give you some things to think about as we find out how the Bible can help you address some of the most important issues in life.

PART IV

APPLYING GODLY WISDOM IN KEY AREAS OF YOUR LIFE

Godly Wisdom for Pride and Anger
Godly Wisdom for Self-discipline and
Developing Friendships

.

Dealing with those ugly twins of pride and anger.

There are many specific issues that can impact your freedom from addiction. In chapters 10 and 11, we will look at four of the primary ones. No one is immune from these problems, and it would be helpful for all Christians to look Biblically at the issues of pride, anger, self-discipline and personal relationships.

There are a lot of people in prison today because they acted impulsively in anger that was brought on by their pride. There are others who were drawn into bad situations because of their lack of self-discipline, or by the friends they kept.

God shows us how to avoid these problems. As you act on His counsel, you will be free from the temptation to return to addictive thinking.

So, open your heart, let down your pride, and read what God has to say about these issues.

Godly Wisdom for Pride and Anger

Chapter 10

A man's pride will bring him low,
but the humble in spirit will retain honor.
Proverbs 29:23

Is pride a positive or negative trait? How should you deal with it?

Pride is a real issue. Many people have been drawn into confrontation because of their pride. I have seen fights break out in prison over someone sitting in another man's chair in the day room or taking another man's ink pen. These fights aren't about chairs or pens; they are about pride.

Others struggle with self-confidence and engage in addictive actions in order to fit in, to cure their shyness or to pretend that they were someone else for a short period. Believing that drugs, booze or bad relationships would add something to their self-image, they were led into an addiction that would eventually control their lives.

It is tempting to see pride and self-esteem as the solutions to these problems. Most non-Christians believe that pride is a good thing. It is considered to be the opposite of shame, and it is used to motivate people to work harder, study more, improve their grades, clean up their home, wash their car and fix most anything else that needs improving. "Have some pride in your work man. Finish the job that you started!" "Take pride in yourself. Don't you care what people think about you?"

Many Christians also consider pride to be a godly motivator and a good character trait. As you will see, the Bible has some surprising things to say about the issue of pride, and God's Word provides a deeper meaning for your true value and greater motivation for self improvement.

Augustine called pride the "love of one's own excellence," which is not necessarily a good thing. Various dictionary definitions call it "the proper sense of one's self worth," "an inordinate view of one's own worth," "the feeling of happiness one enjoys after an accomplishment." No wonder people are confused about this issue. What does the Bible say?

> *These six things the LORD hates, yes, seven are an abomination to Him: A proud look, a lying tongue, Hands that shed innocent blood, a heart that devises wicked plans, Feet that are swift in running to evil, a false witness who speaks lies, and one who sows discord among brethren. Proverbs 6:16-19*

> *Everyone proud in heart is an abomination to the LORD; though they join forces, none will go unpunished. Proverbs 16:5*

Ouch! It would seem that God is not in agreement with the popular view of the value of pride.

The Hebrew word translated as "pride" in Proverbs 6:17 means "to rise, to exalt self, to promote." The word translated as "pride" in Proverbs 16:5 is similar; it means "a lofty look." When either word is applied to a person, the Bible treats it as a negative character trait. The passage in Proverbs 6:16-19 addresses "a proud look," while the one in Proverbs 16:5 addresses those who are "proud in heart." It appears that God hates pride inside and out.

Read Isaiah 14:12-15, and you will see that pride led to Lucifer's downfall.

> *How you are fallen from heaven, O Lucifer, son of the morning! How you are cut down to the ground, you who weakened the nations! For you have said in your heart: 'I will ascend into heaven, I will exalt my throne above the stars of God; I will also sit on the mount of the congregation On the farthest sides of the north; I will ascend above the heights of the clouds, I will be like the Most High.' Yet you shall be brought down to Sheol, to the lowest depths of the Pit. Isaiah 14:12-15*

Lucifer thought that he was equal with God; he even fancied that he was above God, and his pride sent him to the lowest depths. If left unchecked, our pride will mislead us and lead to our downfall as well.

A man's pride (arrogance) will bring him low, but the
humble in spirit will retain honor. Proverbs 29:23

The message of modern psychology is that pride will lift you up. The Bible says that it will bring you low. According to the scriptures, it is the humble in spirit who retain their honor. Another translation says that the humble in spirit *obtain* honor. Thank God for humility; it is the way to honor.

So, true honor is not rooted in pride; true honor is rooted in true humility. What does it mean to be humble? One *Beyond Addictions* student described humility as "knowing that we are absolutely nothing without God and acting accordingly. Humility is obedience to God because of knowing what He has done for you and what He has delivered you from." This is the person that God honors, one who realizes their complete need for Him and their lack of worth without Him. In John 15:5, Jesus told the disciples "without me you can do nothing." This is our state too. Apart from Jesus, we cannot do anything of value.

God loves you. He isn't opposed to pride in order to beat you down. He is opposed to it because it is a superficial and false means of finding your true value. He has a place of honor for you in His kingdom, and it isn't based upon your self-image. It is based upon His love for you. As we approach Him in humility, we receive His honor.

But we all, with unveiled face, beholding as in a mirror
the glory of the Lord, are being transformed into the same
image from glory to glory, just as by the Spirit of the Lord.
II Corinthians 3:18

Here is some good news. As believers in Jesus Christ, we are changed more and more into His image as we spend time with Him. I would much rather take on the image of Jesus than anything that I can dream up in my own pride.

The truth is that God wants to set you free from the false promises of pride. If you have been trying to impress Him with your abilities or your holiness, then stop and admit that you cannot do anything without Him. On this basis, your heart is opened to receive from Him all that you need.

If you have been searching for your true identity by puffing your-self up in pride, remember what Jesus said in the Book of Matthew:

He who finds his life will lose it, and he who loses his life for My sake will find it. Matthew 10:39

You will not find your real purpose or your real identity by build-ing yourself up in pride. The key to finding your real purpose, your real identity, is to give your life to Jesus Christ. Most people do not know who they are until they surrender their life to Jesus. Then they begin to see themselves in the light of Jesus' love and grace. They realize that their true value is found in living for Him. Is there anything more worthwhile than this?

The solution to a poor self-image is not to become more prideful. The solution is to find your life in Jesus Christ.

What else does the Bible say about pride?

The LORD will destroy the house of the proud (arro-gant) but He will establish the boundary of the widow. Proverbs 15:25

Before destruction the heart of a man is haughty, and before honor is humility. Proverbs 18:12

Pride goes before destruction, and a haughty spirit be-fore a fall. Proverbs 16:18

Pride is very misleading. We thought that it would exalt us to the highest heights, but the Bible says that it will bring us low, lead to our destruction and cause us to fall.

You can see the effects of pride and humility in the lives of profes-sional athletes and other celebrities. Living in the public eye, they have the opportunity to boost their own reputation or to live honorably in genuine humility. Listening to some post-game interviews, you will often hear a player take credit for the team's victory or for his own abil-ities. Puffed up in pride, he has forgotten that all of the coaches and players had a role in the team's performance. After all, this is only one game in a long season, and fooled by his pride, this player is setting himself up for a fall in future contests. All it takes is a slight injury or a lack of concentration for him to become an average player, or one mistake to be the goat rather than the hero.

The other night, I watched a major league player hit the winning home run in the bottom of the ninth inning and heard him proclaim how thrilled he was to pull the team through. The next night I saw him strike out four times, once in the bottom of the ninth with the tying run on second base. He went from being the hero to the goat in one night. Pride will cause you to make foolish remarks.

There is a line in Rudyard Kipling's famous poem "If" that summarizes the correct attitude toward life's victories and defeats:

"If you can meet with triumph and disaster
And treat those two imposters just the same."

Triumph and disaster can be deceiving. The humble man doesn't get too headstrong in victory, nor is he crushed in defeat. As we walk in humility through both, God is glorified, and you receive honor from Him. In success, it is important to remember that it was God who gave you the talent in the first place, and He provided the opportunity for you to use it. In defeat, it helps to recall that God is still on the throne and that life's defeats can teach us some of the greatest lessons. In either case, humility will bring honor, and pride will lead to downfall.

Pride also interferes with your ability to learn and to grow.

Do not be wise in your own eyes; Fear the LORD and depart from evil. Proverbs 3:7

The way of a fool is right in his own eyes, But he who heeds counsel is wise. Proverbs 12:15

You may have heard the old saying, "Don't let pride get in the way." Well, it does get in the way. It prevents you from receiving instruction from the Lord and from people who are wiser than you. Pride is the reason that some men stop attending Bible Study; something taught from God's Word has bumped against their pride, and they don't want to hear anymore. At that point, their growth stops.

Pride will lock a baseball player into being a .200 hitter. He refuses to listen to advice from the coach because he believes that he knows best. If he would drop his pride and listen, he might learn something that would enable him to hit .300.

> *The wise in heart will receive commands, but a prating fool will fall. Proverbs 10:8*

> *Every way of a man is right in his own eyes, but the LORD weighs the hearts. Proverbs 21:2*

Continuing the athletic analogy, the best players are usually the ones who are teachable and work hard. Those are the athletes who accomplish the most with their abilities and contribute the most to their teams. The uncoachable ones become the prating or chattering fools of Proverbs 10:8, and they eventually fall.

The bottom line in these four passages is that we learn and grow when we are humble, and we lose that opportunity when we are proud. Pride gets in the way.

Pride causes bitterness and contention.

This is one way that pride clearly contributes to addiction. Satan, your enemy, will often use pride to stir up trouble and then tempt you to relieve the problem with a little medication, a few minutes on an Internet porn site, or a trip to a cheap motel. You may have experienced this on the job when someone was promoted to a position that you believed you deserved. In pride, you harbored anger against the one who made the decision or the one who was promoted. Then Satan began whispering in your ear, "Why don't you just quit," or "Aren't you tired of being mistreated? Let's stop by the bar on the way home." He is a great one for creating a problem and then offering you his brand of relief. You will be free from his trap if you avoid the problem all together. The best way to avoid the problem is to remain humble so that your pride does not lead to strife and violence.

> *By pride comes nothing but strife, but with the well-advised is wisdom. Proverbs 13:10*

> *A proud and haughty man -"Scoffer" is his name; He acts with arrogant pride. Proverbs 21:24*

Pride often leads to violence. The problem usually begins with a petty argument over something that amounts to nothing, a seat at a table, a parking space or a mark on the sidewalk. Then pride enters and the people involved allow the problem to escalate until a fight breaks out. Soon someone is seriously injured or worse. The cause: someone's arrogant pride.

On the other hand, when an arrogant person leaves, strife and violence usually leave with them. You have probably seen this happen at a sporting event or in a prison dorm. Proverbs 22:10 says, *"Cast out the scoffer, and contention will leave; yes, strife and reproach will cease."*

So which is the wise way to act, in pride or in humility?

God is anti-pride.

In *This World: Playground or Battleground*, author A.W. Tozer says, "The effort to appear great will bring the displeasure of God upon us and effectively prevent us from achieving the greatness after which we pant." He goes on to say, "Humility pleases God wherever it is found, and the humble person will have God for his or her friend and helper always. Only the humble are completely sane, for they are the only ones who see clearly their own size and limitations."[17]

> *The fear of the LORD is to hate evil; Pride and arrogance and the evil way and the perverse mouth I hate. Proverbs 8:13*

> *Surely He scorns the scornful, but gives grace (favor) to the humble. Proverbs 3:34*

Do you want to receive God's scorn or His favor? You cannot scoff at other people and expect to receive the favor of God. Lord help all of us to remember this. God's favor is reserved for the humble.

Unfortunately, pride can also be the root cause of our next problem.

---

[17] A.W. Tozer, *This World: Playground or Battleground*, (Camp Hill: Christian Publications, 1989), 34.

How can I avoid becoming angry?

Anger causes all sorts of problems. Tom was a good example of a proud man who created a lot of problems for himself and others through his anger. As a youth, he was diagnosed with extreme schizophrenia, extreme bi-polar disorder, and a number of other problems. There was one thing for sure; he had an extreme anger problem. Eventually, it led him to a prison term of two life sentences.

For most of his life, Tom was fighting with himself. He lived in frustration and stuffed his problems deep inside until they burst to the surface like an angry volcano. The good news is that the problems of pride and anger were solved when he committed his life to Jesus. He is no longer concerned about his self-image; he is concerned about growing in the image of Jesus. He is open and honest before the Lord, so he doesn't stuff his frustrations anymore; He takes them to the cross. His self-control problems have been solved as he submits his life to the leading of the Holy Spirit. He is now Spirit-controlled. Tom was once a poster child for anger management; now he is the epitome of meekness – strength under control.

There are many more men and women like Tom in prison. They were trained to act in anger rooted in a false sense of pride. They have very little concept of self-control until they come face-to-face with Jesus. Then pride begins to melt, and self-control is formed by the work of the Holy Spirit.

In *Proverbs for Today*, Pastor David Hocking states the problem of anger very well, "Bitterness is rooted in the problem of anger. Anger is rooted in the problem of pride. It is our natural tendency and the enemy knows it, so we often need help in dealing with it."[18]

Man has struggled with anger since Cain killed Abel. "Outbursts of wrath" is listed in Galatians 5:20 as a work of the flesh. You will also notice that nothing remotely resembling anger is listed in Galatians 5:22-23 as an aspect of the fruit of the Spirit. So you can safely say that anger is not a work of the Holy Spirit; it is a sinful act of our own flesh. Many of us struggle with this issue.

Anger is also encouraged by demonic forces. You may have seen someone lose all self-control and thought that they were demon-possessed. Well, you may have been right, and you were at least close

---

[18] David Hocking, *Proverbs for Today*, (Promise Publishing Company, 1991)

126

to the truth. You see the results of Satan stoking the fires of a person's anger in cases of extreme violence. Fortunately, the Bible tells us how to deal with this problem.

Why do we become angry?

First of all, you recall from the Book of Proverbs that anger or strife is often rooted in pride.

> *By pride comes nothing but strife, but with the well-advised is wisdom. Proverbs 13:10*

> *He who is of a proud heart stirs up strife, but he who trusts in the LORD will be prospered. Proverbs 28:25*

Notice the contrast. Pride causes strife, but those who think things through are wise. The Bible encourages us to think before we act.

Proverbs 28:25 makes an interesting connection between faith and pride. The contrast in this proverb says that you are not trusting in the LORD if you are proud in heart. So, your pride can interfere with your faith and cause you to act in anger.

> *An angry man stirs up strife, and a furious man abounds in transgression. Proverbs 29:22*

Does this describe you in the past? Does it describe the people you hung around? If so, then you understand where many of your problems started. Your pride has provided Satan with a perfect seedbed for anger and bitterness. As you harbored pride in your heart and acted on it from time to time, you also suffered from it. You may have lost your spouse, been hauled before a judge for domestic violence or lost the respect of your children. Get rid of the pride, anger and bitterness, and you will be much less tempted to lose control. Then you will not have to suffer the consequences.

Two passages in the book of James remind us of where most anger originates.

> *But if you have bitter envy and self-seeking in your hearts, do not boast and lie against the truth. This wisdom*

does not descend from above, but is earthly, sensual, demonic. For where envy and self-seeking exist, confusion and every evil thing are there. James 3:14-16

Where do wars and fights come from among you? Do they not come from your desires for pleasure that war in your members? James 4:1

Again, notice that bitter envy and strife is not of the Lord. It is earthy, sensual and demonic. James 4:1 says that the anger we experience toward each other within the body of Christ is caused by our own personal lust. We want something that we don't have or we want something done our way, and that causes anger, division and fighting, even within the body of Christ.

We cannot claim that our anger is godly or that it comes from above. We are simply fighting to have things our way. We struggle inwardly and act outwardly against those around us, and the turmoil caused by our own lust creates strife, confusion, anger and violence. That doesn't sound like something we need to be about in the body of Christ.

Anger can also lead us back into addiction. In anger we grow in frustration, and we are encouraged to seek a solution to this problem from a bottle or a pill or some other addictive substance. Bars are filled with people who are trying to drink away their frustration and anger.

James 3:15 says that this kind of thinking is demonic. In other words, it is influenced by demonic forces that stir up our own self-seeking desires. If you eliminate the lust in your heart, then the enemy cannot use it to stir you to anger. Remember, we are not wrestling against flesh and blood, but against principalities, against powers, against the rulers of darkness of this age, against spiritual wickedness in high places (Ephesians 6:12).

Acting impulsively rather than controlling our thoughts and actions can also trigger anger. Two passages from the fourteenth chapter of Proverbs explain the problem and remind us that there is great blessing in being slow to become angry.

He who is slow to wrath has great understanding, but he who is impulsive exalts folly. Proverbs 14:29

A wise man fears and departs from evil, but a fool rages and is self-confident. Proverbs 14:16

If you cannot rule your own spirit, then you are open to attacks that cause you to lose control. The Bible likens a man without self-control to a city that has no protection against its enemies.

Whoever has no rule over his own spirit is like a city broken down, without walls. Proverbs 25:28

It is easier to subdue an outward enemy than one within your own heart. Matthew Henry, the great 17th century theologian, was once quoted as saying, "The conquest of ourselves and over our unruly passions requires more true wisdom and a more steady, constant management than obtaining victory of the fires of an enemy. It is harder and therefore more glorious to quash an insurrection at home than to resist an invasion from abroad."[19]

On the other hand, if you allow the Lord to change your thinking and become slow to wrath, you are better than the mighty who take a city.

He who is slow to anger is better than the mighty, and he who rules his spirit than he who takes a city. Proverbs 16:32

These are excellent memory verses that can keep you from losing control when you are confronted with difficult situations. A man of understanding holds his peace and is slow to wrath. Rarely is it intelligent to become angry, and rarely does anger result in anything positive.

Let's look at three explanations for most outburst of anger.

When you seek revenge.

Revenge is a killer. Whenever you have been wronged, the enemy will tempt you to repay the one who mistreated you. The Bible says

---

[19] Matthew Henry, *Matthew Henry's Commentary on the Whole Bible: Volume 3*, Christian Classics Ethereal Library, www.ccel.org/ccel/henry/mhc.i.html.

that it isn't your job to seek revenge. It's God's job, and you may have noticed that we don't perform this job very well.

Do not say, "I will recompense evil"; Wait for the LORD, and He will save you. Proverbs 20:22

Repay no one evil for evil. Have regard for good things in the sight of all men. If it is possible, as much as depends on you, live peaceably with all men. Beloved, do not avenge yourselves, but rather give place to wrath; for it is written, "Vengeance is Mine, I will repay," says the Lord. Romans 12:17-19

When tempted to take revenge, remember instead to wait on the Lord. It isn't our place to take revenge. Later you will find out how to eliminate the bitterness that can cause you to react in revenge.

When you believe that others are treated better than you.

You probably recall the story of the prodigal son in the book of Luke. Most of the attention in this parable is given to the father's love and forgiveness for his son. Thank God for his forgiveness. There is also an account at the end of the story that deserves some attention. It focuses on the older brother's refusal to forgive and his reason for being angry with his father and younger brother.

"But he (the older brother) was angry and would not go in. Therefore his father came out and pleaded with him. "So he answered and said to his father, 'Lo, these many years I have been serving you; I never transgressed your commandment at any time; and yet you never gave me a young goat, that I might make merry with my friends. But as soon as this son of yours came, who has devoured your livelihood with harlots, you killed the fatted calf for him.' "And he said to him, 'Son, you are always with me, and all that I have is yours. It was right that we should make merry and be glad, for your brother was dead and is alive again, and was lost and is found.'" Luke 15:28-32

The older brother had stayed home as the faithful son all those years and felt that his service was not rewarded. In addition, he had no grace in his heart for his lost brother. When his brother repented and returned home, he was incensed, torqued, peeved, and just plain mad. Rather than rejoicing with his father, he refused to go to the party. He felt that his little brother was receiving better treatment than he had been given, and he was not happy about it.

Essentially, the older brother was crying, "It's not fair!" Human nature screams this from the bottom of his soul and from ours. This three-word sentence is probably the first one spoken by most children. It is as if we have been pre-programmed to protect our own interest, and we are pricked in our heart when it is threatened. As fallen men, we tend to hang on to this feeling even as we get older. We tend to become angry when we feel slighted. Watch out. This attitude will carry you to the grave if you do not recognize it, confess it and ask the Lord to help you with it

My own sense of fair treatment gets put in proper perspective when I consider what I deserve from the Lord. Because of my sin, I deserve death. Any treatment less harsh than death is a gift from God, an act of His wonderful mercy. Compared to my sin against the Lord, what is a little offence that someone may have committed against me? Or who cares if someone else received a nicer gift or better treatment than me?

Here is a little warning. Most of us could relate to the younger "prodigal" son when we first accepted Christ. We knew we needed grace, and we were thankful to receive it. As we get older, we run the risk of becoming more like the older son who was judgmental and became angry when grace was extended to someone he felt was less deserving. God's plea to us is then to "remember therefore from where you have fallen; repent and do the first works." Remember grace.

When you become bitter.

Bitterness will affect every thought and action if you let it. You probably know someone who harbors bitterness and is constantly stirring up trouble.

A wrathful man stirs up strife, but he who is slow to anger allays contention. Proverbs 15:18

In Colossians, the Apostle Paul warns you to get rid of the anger, wrath and malice that may have plagued you in the past.

> *But now you yourselves are to put off all these: anger, wrath, malice, blasphemy, filthy language out of your mouth. Colossians 3:8*

He also had to address this problem with the Christians in Ephesus.

> *Let all bitterness, wrath, anger, clamor, and evil speaking be put away from you, with all malice. Ephesians 4:31*

As you can see, the problems of bitterness, wrath and anger are not new; Christians have been dealing with them for centuries. However, they are sinful so they aren't excusable either.

So how can you control your anger?

First of all, follow the leading of the Holy Spirit. The Holy Spirit is THE one who can give you real self-control. In fact, self-control is a supernatural outcome of living under the direction of the Holy Spirit. This is one outcome that you and I need every day.

> *But the fruit of the Spirit is love, joy, peace, longsuffering, kindness, goodness, faithfulness, gentleness, self-control. Against such there is no law. Galatians 5:22-23*

As you live in submission to the Holy Spirit, He provides supernatural grace. He instills in you His love, His joy, His peace, longsuffering, kindness, goodness, faithfulness, gentleness and ... self-control.

Notice that the first aspect of the fruit of the Spirit is love. Every other grace in this list flows from God's love. The fruit or evidence of the Holy Spirit in your life and mine comes as a result of abiding in the love of God. It is God's love that enables us to forgive others and to overcome anger.

I cannot manufacture God's love; I can't even mimic it. Thank God that I can ask Him to fill me with His love for the people around me, and He gives me the genuine article. When I open my heart to receive the love of God, it flows out to the men I minister to in prison, to the guy who cuts me off on the freeway or to the one who has refused to forgive me. Ask and you will receive.

Proverbs 10:12 reminds us of the differing effects of love and hatred.

Hatred stirs up strife, But love covers all sins.
Proverbs 10:12

Love covers all sins. This verse can also be translated "...love overwhelms all sins." God's love overwhelms our sins, and through us, His love can overwhelm the sins that others have committed against us. When we submit ourselves to the Holy Spirit, we walk in love, and like our Lord, we are slow to anger and exhibit self-control.

This is so important. God's love enables us to live free from the anger and hatred and bitterness of the past. I thank God for giving me the opportunity to lay aside the frustration and anger that was natural for me to walk in before I received Jesus Christ. By the power of the Holy Spirit, I have been made free from anger and the host of temptations that usually follow it. You can be set free too.

When we find that we have failed and lost self-control, God makes a way for us to take our sin to Him and be forgiven. Confess your sins and you will receive mercy. Then we can return to walk in His love and grace.

The second thing that you need to do is practice forgiveness. Maybe you have not experienced this sense of freedom in the Holy Spirit. You can, and God wants to set you free from this anger and bitterness. He will enable you to do it through His power to forgive.

First, you need to know that *you* can be forgiven. You may have committed some terrible sins. I work with men who are guilty of murder, sexual assault and other acts of violence. When they come to Christ, they have two problems. The first one is believing that they can be forgiven. The other is forgiving themselves.

The great Apostle Paul led a life of hatred for Jesus before he was saved. In fact, he kicked down doors in the homes of Christians and condemned them to death, sometimes participating in their stoning. Jesus forgave this man and put him in ministry.

Have you ever killed someone because they claimed to be a Christian? Probably not. Even if you have, Jesus can forgive you. The Bible teaches you and me that we can be forgiven for everything we have ever done wrong. This forgiveness and reconciliation with God is made possible by the blood of Jesus Christ, the Son of God who took the wrath that you and I deserved. I John 1:7-9 says that, as believers in Jesus, we have been cleansed of all sin and all unrighteousness.

> *But if we walk in the light as He is in the light, we have fellowship with one another, and the blood of Jesus Christ His Son cleanses us from all sin. If we say that we have no sin, we deceive ourselves, and the truth is not in us. If we confess our sins, He is faithful and just to forgive us our sins and to cleanse us from all unrighteousness. I John 1:7-9*

If God can forgive you, then you can also forgive yourself. You may be surprised by the sinfulness and evil of your actions. You may think, *I can't believe that I did that. I am such a wretched, terrible person.* Let me tell you a little secret: God is not surprised. He was aware of your sinful nature. He already knew about every sinful act you would commit, and He did everything necessary to forgive you. So give it up.

Your struggle to forgive yourself probably has a little to do with personal shame and a whole lot to do with personal pride. Face the facts. Apart from Jesus Christ, you and I are sinners who are capable of terrible evil; however, because of the blood of Jesus, we are forgiven. Due to the work of the Holy Spirit in us, we are capable of incredible acts of love and forgiveness. That is an example of what God can do to change someone from the inside out.

What about our need to forgive others? You need to understand that the debt we owed God was much greater than any that has ever been owed to us. People may have stolen from you, robbed you of your dignity and mistreated you. They may have left you for dead. You may have suffered terribly at the hands of other people, and you are wondering how God can help you cope with the bitterness and pain?

It is hard to grasp right now, but the sins that you and I committed against God were greater than anything that anyone has ever done to us. So, if God can forgive you and me, then He can enable us to forgive them too.

There is a short verse in the book of Ephesians that will help you extend God's forgiveness to others and set you free from the shackles of bitterness.

And be kind to one another, tenderhearted, forgiving one another, just as God in Christ forgave you. Ephesians 4:32

This is one of the most freeing passages in scripture. The Greek word for "forgiving" is the same word used for grace. So, the verse can be interpreted, "Be kind to one another, tenderhearted, gracing another, just as God in Christ also graced you." What is grace? It is a free gift. By grace we have received forgiveness that we do not deserve. By grace, we can give others the kindness we feel that they don't deserve either.

What did you or I do to earn forgiveness from God? Nothing. He did not ask us to jump over one hurdle or to run one step in order to be forgiven of our sins. The verse in Ephesians tells you to extend the same grace to those who have mistreated you. Don't ask them to jump any hurdles; they might not do it, and you will be stuck in bitterness. Don't ask them to pay back the money they owe or to mend the hearts that they broke. Just ask God to give you the supernatural grace to forgive them the way that you have been forgiven.

Once you extend forgiveness, you are free from the pain that it has caused, and the enemy will not be able to torment you with it any longer.

Forgive. Forgive. Forgive. Let go of the anger. Holding onto hatred and unforgiveness hurts you more than anyone. H.E. Fosdick, the early 20th century Baptist and Presbyterian pastor once said, "Hating people is like burning down your own house to get rid of a rat." You may get rid of the rat, but you will destroy your home in the process.

God enables you and me to overlook the wrongs that have been done to us. He empowers us by the Holy Spirit to let go of the pain and hurt so that we never have to be held in bondage to it again. When you let go of the pain and unforgiveness, you also cut the cord that Satan has used to hold you captive to his will.

Conclusion

Allow the Lord to transform you by renewing your mind, and you will be changed from the inside out. Instead of being motivated by your pride, you will be motivated by God's love for you and your desire to abide in Him. As a result, you will do your work as unto the Lord; you will love your spouse as Christ loved the church; you will esteem others as being greater than yourself; you will become a representative of Jesus Christ because He lives in you. You will be able to walk in joy and peace.

When you let go of your pride, you also let go of the reasons for becoming angry. You don't have to defend your reputation because your life is hidden in Christ. You are able to forgive others because you know how much God has forgiven you.

The Holy Spirit abides in you and leads you, so you are free from temptation to become angry. The cord that bound you to abuse and addiction has been broken. No longer a puppet of Satan, you are a child of God, and He will use you to help set others free.

Godly Wisdom for Self-discipline and Developing Friendships

Chapter 11

The steady discipline of friendship with Jesus results in men becoming like Him.
H.E. Fosdick

In the last lesson, we looked into the Bible to see what it says about pride and anger. In this chapter, we will look for Godly advice regarding self-discipline and friendships. The way in which you deal with these two issues will either bless you in freedom or be used by the enemy to enslave you again in addiction.

The Importance of Self-discipline

It is absolutely true that you are saved eternally the minute that you accept Jesus Christ. You are born again by the Holy Spirit at that moment. That doesn't require discipline on your part; it is a work of the Holy Spirit. However, just as a new born baby grows and develops through a process over time, you also grow spiritually through a process over time. The process is called sanctification. It means that you are being trained to be more and more like Jesus. As the Apostle Paul says in Romans 8:29, you are being conformed into the image of Jesus Christ. This growth process requires discipline and effort.

Self-discipline is a Godly trait; the Lord uses it in your life to train you in righteousness. Through self-discipline, you are able to maintain focus on Christ and to lead a fruitful life. By applying self-discipline in your spiritual growth, you will remain free from temptations to return to the addictions and other sins of the past.

In *Conformed to His Image*, Dr. Kenneth Boa stresses the importance of discipline in our relationship with Jesus.

> "There is no growth in the Christian life apart from discipline and self-control ... Spirituality is not instantaneous or haphazard; it is developed and refined. The Epistles

are full of commands to believe, obey, walk, present, fight, reckon, hold fast, pursue, draw near, and love ... You and I will not wake up one morning to find ourselves suddenly spiritual ... We grow in godliness as we hear and obediently respond to the Word."[20]

Christian growth comes as we follow the leading of the Holy Spirit, pray, read the Bible, and do what it says. Growth is both divine and human. God initiates the actions – He saves, He convicts of sin, He sanctifies. We respond because of the effect that Jesus has on our lives – we obey, we pray, we walk in the Spirit, we persevere. There is no spiritual growth without the involvement of both the initiator and the responder. God is always ready to do His part. In this section, we will see a little of what is required for us to do ours.

Tony Dungy was a great and Godly football coach for the Tampa Bay Buccaneers and the Indianapolis Colts. His players knew what was expected of them: to pay attention, work hard, apply the lessons they were learning and to diligently correct their mistakes.

When Coach Dungy arrived in Tampa Bay, they had the worst team record in the NFL, and they had the poorest facilities. He gave the team a list of reasons why they could have another losing season and explain to the world why they failed. Then he erased the list and said that they weren't going to do it that way. Instead, Coach Dungy instilled a new philosophy, "No excuses. No explanations."

Maybe you grew up with situations that provide ready-made explanations for failure. No one in your family ever finished school. You were abused as a child. You never knew your father. You grew up in a series of foster homes. You only have an eighth grade education. You are the only Christian in your family.

So you can pull one of these explanations out anytime you need them, or you can take Coach Dungy's philosophy, "No excuses. No explanations," and find ways to succeed. It requires discipline and commitment. It also requires the same type of faith that Abraham had to patiently endure, to work, to do the right thing simply because it is the right thing to do.

---

[20] Kenneth Boa, *Conformed to His Image*, (Grand Rapids: Zondervan, 2001), 76.

Imagine what you can accomplish in a year or two if you begin applying this philosophy today.

Diligence in our relationship with God leads to real spiritual growth and eternal rewards.

Like other good relationships (marriage, parenting, friendship) our relationship with the Lord requires effort, self-discipline and diligence in order to grow.

> *And we desire that each one of you show the same diligence to the full assurance of hope until the end, that you do not become sluggish, but imitate those who through faith and patience inherit the promises. For when God made a promise to Abraham, because He could swear by no one greater, He swore by Himself, saying, "Surely blessing I will bless you, and multiplying I will multiply you." And so, after he had patiently endured, he obtained the promise.* Hebrews 6:11-15

We live in a fast-paced world with instant oatmeal, instant relief from acid indigestion, microwave everything and high-speed internet access. We want everything now; however, technological advancement hasn't sped up the process of spiritual growth any more than it has sped up the process of growth in a marriage relationship. Both still require time and commitment.

The Bible says that rewards come *after* patient endurance. In this passage, the writer is encouraging us to show diligence until we reach the end, *"that you do not become sluggish but imitate those who through faith and patience inherit the promises."* Then he cites Abraham as an example of one who continued in faith and concludes by saying that it was *after* Abraham patiently endured that he obtained what God had promised him.

Just as you do not lose 20 pounds of fat overnight or add 50 pounds to your maximum on the bench press in a day, you do not instantly achieve spiritual growth. God's plan is for us to learn through experience, through trials, through study of His Word and prayer.

Real growth is a process. Sometimes it is a grinding process, but it yields rich rewards. In order to reap the rewards of walking with God, it is necessary to continue in His service, not to check in and out as you desire, but to continue walking with Jesus, abiding in Him, trusting Him through the trials of the day. As you string together days of trusting the Lord, like Abraham you begin to reap the fruit of patient endurance. It requires self-discipline.

> *Therefore do not cast away your confidence, which has great reward. For you have need of endurance, so that after you have done the will of God, you may receive the promise: For yet a little while, And He who is coming will come and will not tarry. Hebrews 10:35-37*

Starting something is easy; continuing to the end is a different matter. A lot of people will quit when they are discouraged with the results they see in the middle of a trial. They may have believed in the workout regimen when they started, but they aren't seeing their weight fall or their strength increase the way they originally expected. They have grown tired, and it is possible that they haven't stuck to the plan as carefully as they might think. Sometimes all that is required for success is to continue the discipline of showing up. This is true with Christian growth too.

The writer of Hebrews is encouraging us not to throw away the confidence we had when we first believed, but to stick with it. Jesus Christ is changing your life; don't fall away. Whether you see it or not, you are being transformed as you read your Bible and pray. God is continuing the good work that He started when you were saved. You need endurance, particularly on a bad day, in order to continue in the will of God. The full receipt of the promise comes at the end – an eternal home in heaven with Christ, full joy, peace, and complete rest. The Bible assures you that Jesus is coming and that He is a rewarder of those who diligently seek Him (Hebrews 11:6). Remember Galatians 6:9 and *do not grow weary in doing well, in due season, you will reap if you don't quit.*

God desires diligence in our service to Him.

> *Therefore, beloved, looking forward to these things (speaking of the new heavens and new earth), be diligent to*

be found by Him in peace, without spot and blameless; and consider that the longsuffering of our Lord is salvation--as also our beloved brother Paul, according to the wisdom given to him, has written to you. II Peter 3:14-15

The readers of II Peter were looking forward to the return of Jesus. Peter reminds them that this should affect their diligence in their relationship with Jesus and their service to Him until He returns. Are you looking forward to the return of Jesus? If so, then be diligent to be found by Him in peace, without spot and blameless when He returns.

God's principles tell us that He rewards the diligent in this life too.

He who has a slack hand becomes poor, But the hand of the diligent makes rich. Proverbs 10:4

Do you see a man who excels (is diligent) in his work? He will stand before kings; He will not stand before unknown men. Proverbs 22:29

These two passages in Proverbs provide Godly principles for our work. They tell us that diligent workers will be rewarded. They earn more than they would if they were lazy, and they will do their work for kings rather than doing it for unknown men. Have you ever wondered why one contractor renovates million-dollar homes while the other barely gets by? It is possible that the first one is more diligent, works harder to improve his craft, returns phone calls, is on time and simply performs his duties better.

God warns against laziness
A lazy man needs constant supervision in order to accomplish a task. A diligent man does his work as unto the Lord. As a result, he is protected from the results of laziness.

Go to the ant, you sluggard! Consider her ways and be wise, which, having no captain, Overseer or ruler, provides her supplies in the summer, And gathers her food in the harvest. How long will you slumber, O sluggard? When will you rise from your sleep? A little sleep, a little slumber, A little folding of the hands to sleep. So shall your poverty come on you like a prowler, And your need like an armed man. Proverbs 6:6-11

Observe the results of being lazy and learn from them. Turn off the television and get to work. Ants don't need a supervisor to know their duty and to perform it. As a result, they have food to eat in winter. It doesn't take a genius to clearly see the results of laziness, but it does take discipline to work until the job is finished. It is usually the finishers who reap the rewards.

I went by the field of the lazy man, And by the vineyard of the man devoid of understanding; and there it was, all overgrown with thorns; its surface was covered with nettles; its stone wall was broken down. When I saw it, I considered it well; I looked on it and received instruction: A little sleep, a little slumber, A little folding of the hands to rest; So shall your poverty come like a prowler, And your need like an armed man. Proverbs 24:30-34

The writer of Proverbs saw the results of laziness and knew that he did not want his life to be that way. So he was motivated by what he saw to be diligent. We can learn this lesson the same way. Don't think that you have to experience the consequences of foolish or slothful habits in order to learn not to do those things. Learn all you can by observation so that you will not have to experience the sad results firsthand.

A lazy man is not reliable, and he has an excuse for never finishing the job.

As vinegar to the teeth and smoke to the eyes, so is the lazy man to those who send him. Proverbs 10:26

Have you ever sent a lazy man on an errand? If so, you understand the truth in this proverb. You wondered why you didn't just do the job yourself. You can break out of the lazy habit by diligently finishing the next task that you are given. Then make a habit of finishing every task you are given.

Laziness causes the deterioration of the things that you are trying to build into your life.

Because of laziness the building decays, and through idleness of hands the house leaks. Ecclesiastes 10:18

The longer we wait to fix a problem, the bigger the problem becomes until one day, it finally destroys us. This is true about drinking, drugging, pornography, illicit sex, overeating, car trouble, household repairs, you name it. When you see a problem developing, then remember what Barney Fife used to say on the *Andy Griffith Show* and "Nip it, nip it in the bud." A small leak today becomes a downpour tomorrow. A two cigarette a day habit now will be a two pack a day addiction tomorrow. Be diligent to take action before a small problem becomes a big disaster.

Choose which path you want to walk in.

The way of the lazy man is like a hedge of thorns, but the way of the upright is a highway. Proverbs 15:19

The soul of a lazy man desires, and has nothing; but the soul of the diligent shall be made rich. Proverbs 13:4

God's principles in Proverbs tell us that those who are diligent will have a clear path to walk in, and freedom from the thorns and snares of this world. The thorns and snares of this life include broken relationships due to extramarital affairs, loss of employment due to a poor work record, drunkenness, loss of family contact caused by stealing from them to support a drug habit, etc. Through diligence in your commitment to Jesus, you can be free from these and other snares. Diligence leads to blessings that are not available to those who are lazy.

God is glorified and you are blessed when you are diligent.

Bondservants, obey in all things your masters according to the flesh, not with eyeservice, as men-pleasers, but in

sincerity of heart, fearing God. And whatever you do, do it heartily, as to the Lord and not to men, knowing that from the Lord you will receive the reward of the inheritance; for you serve the Lord Christ. But he who does wrong will be repaid for what he has done, and there is no partiality.
Colossians 3:22-25

Have you ever worked in a place where the employees were diligent only when the supervisor was looking? This is a lousy way to spend your day; time drags, and very little work is accomplished. Paul encourages all of us to perform our daily work as if we were employed directly by the Lord. Therefore, we are to do our work heartily or with enthusiasm because we are serving the Lord as we work for others. Some may see this scripture as a liability, but it is really liberating. It is much more enjoyable and much more profitable in the long run to do your work as unto the Lord regardless of who is looking over your shoulder. It sets you free to work well, regardless of whether the boss is watching or not.

Christians should be the best employees in the organization. We should be the most honest, diligent and focused people on the payroll. We should be the ones who make it to work on time every day, even when it snows. Why? God is glorified when you are diligent, when you do your work with the attitude that you are doing it for Him. Make this your goal and do your work every day as unto Jesus, regardless of who notices and regardless of whether you ever receive recognition for it. You will end the day knowing that you have done your best and that you have represented the Lord well.

Choose your friends carefully; they can change your life.

You are shaped by the people you spend the most time around. An old adage says that you are known by the friends you keep. Another old saying is that "birds of a feather flock together" We realize that friendships are important, but you may not realize how significantly they impact every part of your life. That is why it is important to start each day with Jesus, to spend all day abiding in Him and to build relationships with Godly people who can encourage and counsel you to grow in Christ. Let's see what the Bible says about choosing good friends.

The Bible says that friendship is a good thing.

Two are better than one, Because they have a good reward for their labor. For if they fall, one will lift up his companion. But woe to him who is alone when he falls, For he has no one to help him up. Again, if two lie down together, they will keep warm; But how can one be warm alone? Though one may be overpowered by another, two can withstand him. And a threefold cord is not quickly broken. Ecclesiastes 4:9-12

God created us with a desire to have fellowship with each other; we are social beings. This can be a real blessing. Thank God for partners in marriage, in work, and in ministry. We work better together when we encourage one another. Choose your marriage partner and your closest friends carefully. They can pick you up when you are down and deliver you from the enemy when you are tempted.

The "threefold cord" mentioned in this passage includes two earthly partners and the One who makes all of our relationships work. When Jesus is involved in the relationship, the bond is strong, and it is not easily broken.

Friendship with the world is not a good thing.

Adulterers and adulteresses! Do you not know that friendship with the world is enmity with God? Whoever therefore wants to be a friend of the world makes himself an enemy of God. James 4:4

The Bible makes it clear that we cannot indulge the flesh and still claim to love the Lord. James 4:4 is very clear, *"Whoever therefore wants to be a friend of the world makes himself an enemy of God."*

Galatians 6:8 explains the results of being a friend of the world. It says that if we sow to the flesh, we will reap what we sow. We do not want to make the mistake of believing that we can get drunk, shoot up and generally flirt with temptation all week, and then attend church on Sunday and be right with the Lord. What are your highest priorities?

Do your closest friends share the same priorities? Are they interested in following Jesus and going to church, or are they interested in clubbing and chasing men or women?

> *Do not love the world or the things in the world. If anyone loves the world, the love of the Father is not in him. For all that is in the world--the lust of the flesh, the lust of the eyes, and the pride of life--is not of the Father but is of the world. And the world is passing away, and the lust of it; but he who does the will of God abides forever.*
> *I John 2:15-17*

All of those attractive temptations of the world will pass away; they are temporary and they offer no long-term satisfaction. Eternal satisfaction is found in doing the will of God; you will abide forever. Is there enough pleasure in any sin that is worth risking eternal life? Is there any true friend who would want you to risk it? I don't think so.

Too many friends can actually be a problem.

> *A man who has friends must himself be friendly, but there is a friend who sticks closer than a brother.*
> *Proverbs 18:24*

The New American Standard Bible translates this verse, *"He that makes many friends does it to his own destruction; but there is a friend that sticks closer than a brother."* This may be a more accurate translation of Proverbs 18:24, and it means that seeking too many friends can actually be harmful. Have you ever found this to be the case? You may have been tempted to make friends who did you a great deal of harm. At first, they seemed cool; they may have been rich and attractive, exciting and smart. They drew you into friendship, and before you knew it, you were trapped in relationships where they expected you to act against your convictions, or to engage in sinful or even criminal activity based upon your friendship with them. If you seek a relationship with the Lord *first* and let Him direct you, then He will bring you into fellowship with the people who seek to help rather than to harm.

Choose your friends wisely.

He who walks with wise men will be wise, But the companion of fools will be destroyed. Proverbs 13:20

The righteous should choose his friends carefully, For the way of the wicked leads them astray. Proverbs 12:26

Memorize these two verses. I have never read better reasons for carefully choosing friends. First of all, if you associate with wise men, you will become wise. Talking with wise men increases your knowledge, improves your vision and changes your outlook. The world says that you learn from your peers; I believe that you learn most from those who are wiser than you. It is a blessing to have friends with more Godly wisdom than you.

On the other hand, a companion of fools becomes foolish, and they are eventually destroyed. This is the simple explanation for the failure of some young people who were on the right track and then took a detour. Last year they were on the honor roll at school and active in church. Then they started hanging around the wrong crowd at the park or the game room, and their grades begin to slip, along with their morals. Now they are considering dropping out of school, and they wouldn't be caught dead inside of a church building. What happened? Proverbs 13:20 and 12:26 explain it; they were influenced by fools.

Who is influencing you? Are they wise men or women who can lead you upward, or are they unrighteous men or women who will take you down with them? Make sure that you are investing time with the right influencers.

Read the following passages and see if they describe any of your current relationships.

A perverse man sows strife, and a whisperer separates the best of friends. A violent man entices his neighbor, and leads him in a way that is not good. Proverbs 16:28-29

Make no friendship with an angry man, and with a furious man do not go, lest you learn his ways And set a snare for your soul. Proverbs 22:24-25

Do not be deceived: "Evil company corrupts good habits." I Corinthians 15:33

A former prison inmate once told me that no man ever falls and returns to prison by himself; he has help getting back there. One of your most important commitments regards whom you spend time with. Angry men will drag you into violence. Don't get into the car with them. They will ensnare your soul; they may even help you get to prison. Evil company will corrupt the good habits that you are developing in your life; stay away from the gangs or groups that corrupt your life.

The Bible tells you to flee sexual sin (I Corinthians 6:18), flee idolatry (I Corinthians 10:14), flee covetousness (I Timothy 6:11) and to flee youthful lusts (II Timothy 2:22). If someone claiming to be your friend is trying to drag you back into any of this, then flee them; get out!

What is true about friends is even truer when you are considering a spouse.

We are not focusing on marriage relationships in this chapter, but it is too important to ignore when you are talking about friendships. The second most important relationship in your life is with your spouse; the first is with Jesus. Marriage should not be entered into lightly, nor should you enter into and exit marriage at your own will.

Do not be unequally yoked together with unbelievers.
For what fellowship has righteousness with lawlessness?
And what communion has light with darkness?
II Corinthians 6:14

This passage applies to a lot more than marriage, but it certainly applies there first. Do not be unequally yoked with unbelievers. It is not God's design for you to enter into marriage with an unbeliever. Now, if you are already married, then His counsel is to remain so.

You should not choose your spouse based upon their personal appearance or shared interests. Looks change and personal interests are too thin to build a marriage upon. The primary shared interest that you must have with your prospective mate is Jesus Christ. He has a way of cementing relationships when our eyes are on Him and our devotion is for Him.

Secondly, your spouse should be your closest friend next to Jesus. Do not make the mistake of sharing stories or jokes with your buddies that you would not take home to your wife or husband. No earthly being should be more important to you than your spouse. When the Pharisees asked Jesus about divorce, He quoted Genesis.

> *And He answered and said to them, "Have you not read that He who made them at the beginning 'made them male and female,' "and said, 'For this reason a man shall leave his father and mother and be joined to his wife, and the two shall become one flesh'? "So then, they are no longer two but one flesh. Therefore what God has joined together, let not man separate." Matthew 19:4-6*

"One flesh" is a pretty close relationship. There is no other relationship in the Bible that is described this way. Seek Godly counsel if you are considering marriage or if you are experiencing trouble in your marriage. This bond between a man and a woman is the second most important relationship in the world. God uses it as an earthly illustration of the relationship between Jesus Christ and the church. Marriage should be seriously considered before entering into it, and it should be protected once it is begun.

Conclusion

In the last two chapters, we have examined more than 50 scripture passages related to these four topics: 1) How to deal with pride, 2) How to avoid becoming angry, 3) The importance of self-discipline and 4) Choosing your friends carefully. These are four important issues as you move beyond addictions to live free in Christ Jesus. Read your Bible, and you will find that there are many verses that address these and other key points that will enable you to grow closer to Jesus and keep you free from slavery to addictions.

God's Word is able to make you wise in every area of life. You can trust it, and you can depend upon the Lord to use it to direct your steps, whether the issues relate to addictions or any other area of life. Read it. Study it. Apply it. Continue in it, and you will remain free.

PART V

BUILDING WALLS OF PROTECTION TO CONTINUE WINNING THE SPIRITUAL BATTLES AGAINST ADDICTION

The Eternal Construction Project
Continuing the Work of Jesus Christ
Completing the Good Work that He Has Begun in You
Putting it All to Work

You are Involved in an Eternal Construction Project

God is building something special in your life. He is transforming you as your mind is renewed by the Word of God and the Holy Spirit, and He is conforming you more and more into the likeness of Jesus Christ. He has also promised to finish the work that He has begun in you. This is a lifelong project. Thank God that He didn't leave us on our own to get the job done.

In the next three chapters, you will see how God enabled the people of Israel to rebuild the walls of Jerusalem while under attack from the enemy. You will also see how He is building your life to protect you from Satan, your enemy, who seeks to kill you, steal from you, and destroy you. The people of Israel were successful in their project. You will be successful too as you follow the direction that the Lord gives you through His Word.

The Eternal Construction Project

Chapter 12

"Building walls of protection in Christ, these lessons are very important to me. I have learned that without this protection, the enemy can walk in any time and tear down what I am trying to build. Without God's protection, I am very vulnerable, so I must keep the communication lines open to God, and I cannot let the devil take up space in my head."
A.H. – *Beyond Addictions* Graduate 2009

You have started a good work, and you have come a long way since you began studying this book. You are being transformed by the renewal of your mind. You understand addiction is a form of idolatry, voluntary slavery, life-dominating sin and adultery against the Lord. You also know the One who defeated it at the cross and gave you the Holy Spirit to guide you into the new life you have in Christ Jesus.

Having enjoyed some success in the battle, you should not be surprised when the enemy mounts an attack to drag you back into the pit where he once held you captive. He is not happy about your new life in Christ, and he isn't interested in having you draw others out of his trap. So he tempts and he attacks to draw you back or to have you live in fear.

What can you do about it? In order to answer that question, I want to take you back 2,435 years to the time when Nehemiah was serving as chamberlain and advisor to the king of the Medo-Persian Empire. The Jews were returning to Israel, and like you, they were at a critical point of transition. The people of Israel were trying to re-establish themselves in their homeland after seventy years of captivity in Babylon. Their state was similar to yours as you re-establish your freedom after being held captive to addiction.

This is the story of a construction job that God was doing in the City of Jerusalem. It is very similar to the construction job that He is doing in your life. The greatest difference is that yours will last longer. You may think that a literal construction project involving wood and stone would be more real than a spiritual project that goes unseen; however, the truth of the matter is that the spiritual construction project in your life will outlast the one that was completed in Jerusalem. The walls of Jerusalem were effective for a short period of time, but they were destroyed. The Bible teaches that the construction work being done in your spirit and soul will last forever!

By studying this literal construction job in Jerusalem, you will learn a lot about the spiritual one being done in you. Let's examine it to see what we can learn.

During the time of Nehemiah in 444 BC, a city was known by its walls. Walls protected people from enemy armies, thieves and robbers. Gates were closed at night to keep the enemy from creeping in and creating confusion or staging an all out attack. Walls were great defensive barriers during war. If an enemy was going to attack your city, he would first send in spies to find the weaknesses in your walls. Strong walls not only protected a city during attack, they often discouraged the enemy from attacking at all. "The walls are too strong, we can't get through." People who built strong walls were perceived as a mighty people; they were wise, they were skillful, they were highly developed and they had great physical strength.

As strong walls were associated with a strong city and a great people, weak walls were associated with a defenseless city and weak people. If they had any strength, they would have built walls to protect them. So, a lack of strong walls meant that the people were weak, poor, beaten down and easy targets for the enemy.

The same is true today. Satan, your real enemy, knows your strengths and weaknesses. He is looking for lust, pride and other weaknesses in your defenses so that he will know how to tempt, how to attack. He also knows that your only real protection lies in Christ. You can keep the enemy out by continuing to abide in Christ and permitting Him to build a strong foundation in your life. As it says in the book of Colossians,

> *As you have therefore received Christ Jesus the Lord, so walk in Him, rooted and built up in Him and established in the faith, as you have been taught, abounding in it with thanksgiving. Colossians 2:6-7*

You need to get rooted. Dig deep, lay a solid foundation and continue building strong walls to protect you from the attack of the enemy. Do this and you will succeed. Jesus has been building strong lives for centuries as men and women walk in Him.

Now there are men who believe that they are tough enough to withstand Satan on their own, but real strength doesn't lie in pride or self-sufficiency. It doesn't lie in leather, tattoos and bulging muscles either. It is found in Jesus Christ. The enemy recognizes men who trust in their own strength; he knows that they are weak-willed and easy targets for drug addiction, booze and whatever else he wants to throw at them. Do you remember Samson?

Unfortunately, the people of Israel were in a position of real weakness when Nehemiah first heard about their condition.

> *The words of Nehemiah the son of Hachaliah. It came to pass in the month of Chislev, in the twentieth year, as I was in Shushan the citadel, that Hanani one of my brethren came with men from Judah; and I asked them concerning the Jews who had escaped, who had survived the captivity, and concerning Jerusalem. And they said to me, "The survivors who are left from the captivity in the province are there in great distress and reproach. The wall of Jerusalem is also broken down, and its gates are burned with fire." So it was, when I heard these words that I sat down and wept, and mourned for many days; I was fasting and praying before the God of heaven. Nehemiah 1:1-4*

Hanani had returned from Jerusalem to the Persian winter palace at Shushan. Nehemiah was serving the king there, and he was anxious to hear about the Jews who had returned to Israel. As you can see, he was pretty upset with this news from Jerusalem. He had hoped to hear that the people were faring well since returning to the homeland. Ezra had led a group of Israelites back into the land 14 years earlier. This was the second mission that had returned to Israel during the previous 95 years. When Hanani told Nehemiah about the walls, he knew that the people were suffering, weak and beaten down.

You may have experienced something similar. Have you ever known anyone who moved through drug rehabilitation and seemed to be on the right track? Then something began to go south. They stopped attending church regularly. You heard that they lost their job because they weren't coming to work on time. Immediately you knew that the walls of protection had been broken down, and they were open to the attacks of the enemy again.

How should we respond to this kind of news? Nehemiah's response should be our response. He wept, mourned, and he prayed.

Read Nehemiah 1:5-11 and notice the aspects of Nehemiah's prayer:

- He worshipped the Lord (verse 5).
- He confessed his sins and the sins of the people (verses 6-7).
- He interceded for them based upon God's Word, specifically His promises to them (verses 8-9).
- He asked for God to lead him and to bless him as he approached the king (verse11).

How does this apply to your situation? Your first reaction to any situation should be prayer. Victory comes when God intercedes for you. Philippians 4:6-7 reminds us of the power of prayer and its effects in our own soul.

> *Be anxious for nothing, but in everything by prayer and supplication, with thanksgiving, let your requests be made known to God; and the peace of God, which surpasses all understanding, will guard your hearts and minds through Christ Jesus. Philippians 4:6-7*

Do not worry. Pray. Focus on the blessings of the Lord even in the midst of the trial, and the peace of God will guard your heart and mind in Christ. To "guard" literally means that He will build a fortress around your heart and mind, and this is where the spiritual battle is fought.

In chapter four of the Book of James, we are reminded of God's call to humility and prayer.

> *Therefore He says, "God resists the proud, but gives grace to the humble." Therefore submit to God. Resist the devil and he will flee from you. Draw near to God and He*

will draw near to you. Cleanse your hands, you sinners; and purify your hearts, you double-minded. James 4:5-7

In humility, you submit to God. As a result, the devil flees. As you draw near to God, He draws near to you. Cleanse your hands and your hearts in repentance to Jesus Christ. Remember that you are promised in I John 1:9 that God will honor your confession by forgiving you and cleansing you from all unrighteousness.

Pray. Repent. Worship the Lord. Ask for His help.

Nehemiah's Initial Actions

In Nehemiah 2:1-8, you find that after 120 days of prayer, his opportunity came to approach the king. Because of the time spent with the Lord, Nehemiah was prepared and the Lord gave him favor. So Nehemiah's request to go to Jerusalem and rebuild the walls was approved, and he was ready when he received the king's blessing to return to Jerusalem. Having his heart right before God, Nehemiah was prepared. He was "prayed up," and he knew what steps to take next as he operated in the wisdom of the Lord.

> *Then I went to the governors in the region beyond the River, and gave them the king's letters. Now the king had sent captains of the army and horsemen with me. Nehemiah 2:9*

God granted Nehemiah favor in ways that he could not have seen before he took this step of faith. God is going before you too. He will make a way for you to work; He will provide a safe place to live and a good Bible-teaching local church. He will provide for all your needs according to His riches in glory in Christ Jesus.

> *When Sanballat the Horonite and Tobiah the Ammonite official heard of it, they were deeply disturbed that a man had come to seek the well-being of the children of Israel. Nehemiah 2:10*

This is the first mention in Nehemiah of the enemies of Israel. Sanballat and Tobiah noticed that a man had come to seek the well-being of the ones that they had held in bondage, and they weren't happy about it. Your enemy isn't happy about your new life either, and he isn't interested in letting you seek the well-being of the ones you love.

You are going to experience trials in this life. Let me share something from *Jesus Calling* by Sarah Young. This message is written as if it was being spoken directly to you by Jesus:

> Do not long for the absence of problems in your life. That is an unrealistic goal since in this world you will have trouble. You have an eternity of problem-free living reserved for you in heaven. ...
>
> Begin each day anticipating problems asking Me to equip you for whatever difficulties you will encounter. The best equipping is My living Presence. ... Discuss everything with Me. Take a lighthearted view of trouble, seeing it as a challenge that you and I together can handle. Remember that I am on your side, and I have overcome the world.[21]

Even though you experience the favor of God, you will still experience trials and attacks from the enemy. This is a normal part of Christian living. Don't attempt to avoid them; expect them, and remember the promise in I John 4:4, *greater is he that is in you than he who is in the world.* Before Jesus went to the cross, He gave the disciples some reassurance for the trials ahead.

> *These things I have spoken to you, that in Me you may have peace. In the world you will have tribulation; but be of good cheer, I have overcome the world. John 16:33*

The Sanballat-type of troubles are going to show up from time to time. The appearance of the enemy didn't surprise Nehemiah, and it shouldn't surprise you either. God has a plan. Seek His will in times of trials and follow His direction. Not only will He enable you to overcome the difficulties; He will bless you in the process.

In Nehemiah 2:11-16, he describes his arrival at Jerusalem and his tour of the city to see the damage to the wall and gates. Nehemiah didn't make an open show of his actions at this time. He didn't enter

---

[21] Sarah Young, *Jesus Calling*, (Nashville: Thomas Nelson, Inc., 2004), 135.

town with a lot of noise and fanfare. Neither should you. You don't need to announce to the world that you have been rehabilitated and it's different this time. You don't have to sell people on how well you are doing. Just keep your eyes focused on the Lord and follow Him. Then they will see the work that God is doing – transforming you by the renewal of your mind, and conforming you into His likeness by the power of the Holy Spirit. In addition, by maintaining your focus on Jesus, you are less likely to be fooled by the tricks of the enemy. Like Nehemiah, you can simply let the work speak for itself.

As you read through the account in Nehemiah, you will see that one of the keys to his success was his constant focus on the Lord, and on the work that the Lord called him to do. He did not allow the distractions of the enemy or the negative influences in the city affect him. His circumstances did not dictate his thoughts or actions. He allowed his relationship with God to guide him through every situation.

This is crucial. As Christians, God has given you and me the Holy Spirit to do the same for us, and we do not have to allow the situations of our lives to dictate our thoughts or actions either. We serve a God who led David through the wilderness for years and enabled the Jews to rebuild Jerusalem while under enemy attack. He will also guide you through times of difficulty. Follow Him.

In verses 17-18, Nehemiah gave the people of Jerusalem a reality check.

> *Then I said to them, "You see the distress that we are in, how Jerusalem lies waste, and its gates are burned with fire. Come and let us build the wall of Jerusalem, that we may no longer be a reproach." And I told them of the hand of my God which had been good upon me, and also of the king's words that he had spoken to me. So they said, "Let us rise up and build." Then they set their hands to this good work. Nehemiah 2:17-18*

Nehemiah told them the whole truth. Their lives were a mess, and they were living in subjection to an enemy who wanted to destroy them. Maybe they had forgotten how bad the situation was. It's easy for anyone to grow comfortable with misery, to start thinking that addiction is normal and that you will always have to contend with it. Then you fall victim to the whole set of circumstances that go along with addiction: lust, pornography, illicit sex, poor work habits, self-obsession, an all-around sinful lifestyle. As you become more discouraged, your thinking is dulled, and you believe that life will always be that way.

You need the kind of wake up call that Nehemiah gave the Israelites in Jerusalem. Take an inventory of yourself. Are you still entertaining the enemy in your mind through lust? Do you spend time reminiscing about the "fun" you had when you were in addiction? Give up the "little indiscretions" you may be having now with a toke on a joint or an occasional drink. Get rid of the pornography. Face the facts. If these things still exist, you are opening yourself up to more serious problems later. Pray Psalm 139:23-24 to the Lord and ask for His help.

Nehemiah also told them the good news, and you need to know it too. God had given him favor with the king and brought him back to Jerusalem to rebuild. You need to remember that God is on your side, that He will never leave you or forsake you (Hebrews 13:5). Being confident of this very thing that he which hath begun a good work in you will perform it until the day of Jesus Christ (Philippians 1:6). Remember that the blood of Jesus has cleansed you from all sin (I John 1:7), that the Holy Spirit dwells in you (I Corinthians 3:16). You may be in a pickle, but God is able to deliver you out of any addiction and the lifestyle that goes along with it. And II Chronicles 16:9 says that He wants to do it.

> *For the eyes of the LORD run to and fro throughout the whole earth, to show Himself strong on behalf of those whose heart is loyal to Him. II Chronicles 16:9a*

So trust Him with your whole heart and see what He does. If you are a believer, read the foundational verses from this course and remember the good news:

1. You are a new creation in Christ (II Corinthians 5:17)
2. God has given you all you need in the knowledge of Him (II Peter 1:3)
3. You can be completely changed by the renewal of your mind (Romans 12:2)
4. You are under new management and do not need to give in to the fears of the past (I Corinthians 6:19-20)

5. You can defeat temptation by taking thoughts captive (II Corinthians 10:3-5) and take the way out that God provides (I Corinthians 10:13)
6. God is for you (Jeremiah 29:11)
7. Keep the faith, don't quit (Galatians 6:9)

These verses will strengthen your hands, as well as your heart and mind, for the work we need to do. Let's rise up and build!

Read verses 19-20 and note the response of Nehemiah's enemies when they heard of the work he had planned. Then check out his response:

> *But when Sanballat the Horonite, Tobiah the Ammonite official, and Geshem the Arab heard of it, they laughed at us and despised us, and said, "What is this thing that you are doing? Will you rebel against the king?" So I answered them, and said to them, "The God of heaven Himself will prosper us; therefore we His servants will arise and build, but you have no heritage or right or memorial in Jerusalem." Nehemiah 2:19-20*

The enemy laughed at Nehemiah and despised the people. Has the world ever laughed at you and scorned you? You may have heard them say something like this, "Yea, yea, so you're trying this Christian thing now. You'll be back in two weeks." "You're a fool to give up all of this for a bunch of rules and a church full of hypocrites." "What are you going to try after this fails?" Don't let their opinions worry you. Notice how Nehemiah responded to the scorn of the enemy. He looked them in the eye and set the record straight, *"The God of heaven will prosper us, therefore, we his servants, will arise and build."* AMEN!

You do not need to be concerned about the opinions of those who want to drag you back into addiction. The opinion that matters is God's, and since He is in it, the work will succeed. He who has begun a good work in you will complete it. You have the privilege of being called by God to participate in the work that He is doing in you and through you. Since you know that this is His work, you can also be sure that it will succeed. So, arise and build.

If you are reading this book, I believe that you have a desire to clear away the rubble of your past and to build a good foundation for your future. That's good. Now, set the record straight, and don't give Satan, your enemy, any place in your heart to draw you into compromise. Remember Colossians 2:9-10:

For in him dwells all the fullness of the Godhead bodily. And you are complete in him, which is the head of all principality and power.

This isn't a battle that we are leading. Christ is leading the charge, and we are complete in Him. The God of heaven will prosper you in the battle. That is why you can arise, and you will be victorious in building a new life in Him. It is His might, His power and His Spirit that gives the victory. Your responsibility is to be faithful to participate in the work that He is calling you to do, to follow His lead.

Note the last thing that Nehemiah told their enemies, *"but you have no heritage or right or memorial in Jerusalem."*

Remember that Satan, your enemy, has no heritage or right or memorial in you either. Any inheritance he had was lost to him when you surrendered your life to Jesus. Your life does not belong to the devil. You belong to Jesus. You now live by faith in the Son of God who died for you.

Satan has no right in you either; you have been bought by the blood of the Lamb. Your body is now the temple of the Holy Spirit (I Corinthians 6:19). You don't need to respond when Satan reminds you of your past because you are a new creation in Christ Jesus, and those old things are passed away (II Corinthians 5:17).

Satan should have no memorial in you either. This is your responsibility. Get rid of anything that reminds you of the sinful past. Throw out the magazines, the bong pipes, the beer signs and anything else that might remind you of your old ways. Don't leave anything that the enemy can use as a hook to entice you back into sin.

The *Bible Knowledge Commentary* says, "Nehemiah brought the task—both in the eyes of Judah and his enemies—into clear focus. Their dependence was not to be on their abilities, human resources, or personal genius. Their hope was in the God of heaven!"[22] So is yours.

---

[22] John F. Walvoord and Roy B. Zuck, eds., *The Bible Knowledge Commentary: Old Testament*, (Colorado Spring: Cook Communications Ministries, 2004), 677-678.

Let's bring the task into clear focus. Your life is being rebuilt. The enemy who stands against you may be strong, but the God of heaven will empower you to succeed; therefore you will arise and build!

You are building for the future.

This is the most important time in your life. If you build a solid foundation now, you will be able to stand on it the rest of your life.

"Chapters 12 through 14 were foundational to learning how to transition from prison to the outside world. During my first 6 months of release I was amazed at how much I recognized what was going on during my search for housing and a job. The tricks of the enemy were completely laid open by what I learned through these chapters."

John Whitehead – Beyond Addictions Graduate 2007

Continuing the Work of Jesus Christ

Chapter 13

Remember the Lord, great and awesome,
and fight for your brethren, your sons, your daughters,
your wives, and your houses.
Nehemiah 4:14

In chapter 12, you began building walls in Christ to strengthen and protect you from the attack of the enemy. In chapter 13, we will continue the work, and you will begin to see some of the enemy's tactics that he employs to frustrate the good work that the Lord is doing in your life.

Understanding the devices of the enemy.

You seldom have any problem with Satan or with those who run with him until you start going against the flow. As soon as you do, you can expect retaliation. Don't be surprised when the spiritual attack comes, and don't quit. Remember, greater is He that is in you than he that is in the world (I John 4:4).

He will attempt to discourage and ridicule your efforts.

There is a fictional story that reveals some truth about the devices that Satan uses to draw people away from Jesus. It seems that the devil was holding a sale of some of his greatest tools. One of his minions was looking at the bright, shiny articles lined along the wall. Each had a very expensive price tag. These were the tools that his boss had used to bring down billions of people. They included lust, pride, greed, power, the desire for material wealth, and many other tempting items. The prices were high, and no doubt they were worth every penny.

Then the little demon spotted an old stick leaning in the corner, and he walked over to take a look. To his surprise, he saw that it was priced ten times higher than any of the bright, shiny ones. So he asked his evil master why the old stick was worth so much. The devil grinned and said, "This is my most prized possession. It is 'discouragement.' If

I can wedge it into a man's heart, then I can pry it open and pour whatever I want into his life."

You may have experienced this. Moving forward in your new life, you suddenly come face-to-face with discouragement, and you begin thinking about the old ways that you used to escape it in the past. You are tempted to go back to the bar, or to find the drug man, or to look for some momentary pleasure in another way. Don't give in. Take a look at how Nehemiah handled this problem.

Sanballat could not stop the work with his initial actions, so he raised the heat a little. The first thing he did was to ridicule the effort that the Israelites were making to change their circumstances. The goal was to discourage them from even trying to build the wall.

> But it so happened, when Sanballat heard that we were rebuilding the wall, that he was furious and very indignant, and mocked the Jews. And he spoke before his brethren and the army of Samaria, and said, "What are these feeble Jews doing? Will they fortify themselves? Will they offer sacrifices? Will they complete it in a day? Will they revive the stones from the heaps of rubbish-stones that are burned?" Now Tobiah the Ammonite was beside him, and he said, "Whatever they build, if even a fox goes up on it, he will break down their stone wall." Nehemiah 4:1-3

Notice Sanballat's response to the work that the Lord was doing in Jerusalem:

1. He was angry.
2. He mocked the work they were doing.
3. He made fun of their "feeble" effort.
4. He had a friend who joined him (enemies of God seldom stand alone).

Does any of this sound familiar? Maybe you have heard this, "What do you mean, you're moving out? You'll be back, there's no way you can live without it." "Go on down to your little church folk. When they find out what kind of person you really are, they won't have anything to do with you either, and you'll come running back." So don't be surprised; some people are just going to mock the work that the Lord is doing in your life.

How should you respond? How did Nehemiah respond?

> *Hear, O our God, for we are despised; turn their reproach on their own heads, and give them as plunder to a land of captivity! Do not cover their iniquity, and do not let their sin be blotted out from before You; for they have provoked You to anger before the builders. So we built the wall, and the entire wall was joined together up to half its height, for the people had a mind to work.*
> *Nehemiah 4:4-6*

Nehemiah prayed, and he continued doing the work the Lord called him to do. Other than lifting his request to the Lord in prayer, he paid no attention to the ridicule of the enemy. As a result, the work began to succeed. It will succeed with you too.

If Nehemiah had stopped when he was ridiculed, then Sanballat would have known how to stop the work anytime he wanted. All he had to do was throw a little sand in Nehemiah's face, and he would run away. Instead, Nehemiah remained steadfast in the work and prayed for God to defend the people of Israel as they engaged in the work that God desired them to complete.

Satan, your enemy, is a master of discouragement. He will attempt to pry open the door of your mind with this old stick, and then he can pour in most anything that will tempt you to quit. While whispering thoughts of failure or depression in one ear, he will tempt you with his bag of dope or pills or booze or pornography as the solution to the problem. Don't buy into it. Remember the promises of God. Your sins have been forgiven by the blood of Jesus (I John 1:7, 9). He who has started a good work in you will complete it (Philippians 1:6). Jesus will never leave you or forsake you (Hebrews 13:5).

In verse six, you see another reason for the success of the project, *"the people had a mind to work."* Remember the value of self-discipline from the scripture passages we studied in chapter eleven. The message in Hebrews 10:35-36 will put a little steel in your determination:

> *Do not cast away your confidence, which has great re-*
> *ward. For you have need of endurance, so that after you have*
> *done the will of God, you may receive the promise.*
> *Hebrews 10:35-36*

Note that it is *after* you have done the will of God that you receive the promise. You must have a mind to work. Maintain your discipline in Bible reading, prayer and fellowship with solid Christians. Put some praise music in your mp3 player or tune your radio to a good Christian station. Don't play around with "little" sins in your mind. Catch those little tempting thoughts and cast them out before you begin dwelling on them. When the enemy brings temptation to mind, respond with prayer and praise to Jesus. Have a mind to work, and you will succeed.

He will employ confusion.

The Israelites began to succeed. The wall was starting to look more like a wall and less like a pile of rocks and sticks. So the enemies of Israel turned up the heat. When you show some success, your enemy will turn up the heat too.

> *Now it happened, when Sanballat, Tobiah, the Arabs,*
> *the Ammonites, and the Ashdodites heard that the walls of*
> *Jerusalem were being restored and the gaps were begin-*
> *ning to be closed, that they became very angry, and all of*
> *them conspired together to come and attack Jerusalem and*
> *create confusion. Nevertheless we made our prayer to our*
> *God, and because of them we set a watch against them day*
> *and night. Nehemiah 4:7-9*

Sanballat, Tobiah and the boys started focusing more effort on the Israelites. They made plans to attack and to create confusion.

Confusion is another weapon that the enemy uses against those of us who have escaped his prison of addiction. He may actually try to convince you that it was better when you were drinkin', druggin' and running around. Physical cravings may surface for the first time in a long while. He may bring a girlfriend or boyfriend from the old days around to see you. He may tempt you with an R-rated movie. He wants you to wonder if you are missing something. He wants to confuse you.

How should you respond? Like Nehemiah, make your prayer unto God, and set a watch against the enemy day and night. That means all of the time. Remember that Satan is a liar and the father of lies. In John 8:44, Jesus says, *"There is no truth in him. When he speaks a lie, he speaks from his own for he is a liar, and the father of it."*

If you are feeling confused, remember that God is not the author of confusion. When doubt or fear rises in your heart, seek the Lord for clear direction. Sit down with an open Bible and pray. God will hear you, and He will direct your path.

How do we set a watch against the enemy?

Nehemiah established a physical system to guard against enemy attacks. How can you set up a spiritual watch against your enemy? Apply the Word.

1. Take thoughts captive to the obedience of Christ (II Corinthians 10:3-5).
2. Remember that the problem you are facing is due to the enemy tempting a lust in your heart and recall that falling to it will not bring real joy, but it brings death (James 1:14-15).
3. Decide in your heart to be a doer of the Word and not just a hearer. Lay aside all of the evil around you, and in meekness receive God's Word that is able to deliver you (James 1:21-22).
4. Remember the adulterous woman in Proverbs 9 and that the door to her home may look like it leads to pleasure, but it actually leads to death (Proverbs 9:18).
5. Remember the covenant with your eyes, why should you even think upon a maid? (Job 31:1).
6. Focus your eyes on Jesus, the author and finisher of our faith, who for the joy set before Him, endured the cross in order that you and I could be saved (Hebrews 12:2).

These are just six tools that you can use to keep the enemy from entering your mind when he comes calling.

Unfortunately, the laborers took their eyes off of the Lord, so Sanballat and Tobiah's tactics were somewhat effective. As a result, the people became discouraged and confused.

> *Then Judah said, "The strength of the laborers is fail-*
> *ing, and there is so much rubbish that we are not able to*
> *build the wall." Nehemiah 4:10*

Evidently, the workers came out one morning and rather than focusing on their leader and the work that they were called to do, they
began focusing their eyes on the rubbish. There were still piles of broken down stone and wood from the old wall that needed to be removed
before the new wall could be built. Rather than continuing to have a
mind to work and focusing on the Lord, they focused on the piles of
rubbish. As a result, they became discouraged and began to complain.

You may still have some rubbish in your life too, but God is not
telling you to focus on the failures of the past. Hebrews 12:1-2 tells us
how to succeed in our walk of faith. It says, *"Fix your eyes on JESUS."*
This is the key. Your life of faith in Christ leads to success as you dwell
on Him rather than being discouraged and confused by the problems of
the past.

Remember, discouragement and confusion are not new. The enemy
has used these tools for centuries as a means of stopping the servants of
God. David became discouraged at times. Moses, Peter, Paul and many
other great men of faith lost their perspective too. So do we. It generally happens when we take our eyes off of Jesus and focus on our circumstances.

Psalm 1:1-2 provides us with the secret to returning to a place of
personal peace and blessing.

> *Blessed is the man who walks not in the counsel of the*
> *ungodly, nor stands in the path of sinners, nor sits in the seat*
> *of the scornful; but his delight is in the law of the LORD, And*
> *in His law he meditates day and night. Psalm 1:1-2*

The enemy wants you to listen to the advice of the ungodly, to
stand with unbelievers, and to sit with the scornful. He knows that this
will discourage and confuse you. The Bible says that the way to true
happiness is NOT to do these things, but instead to delight in God's
Word, meditating on it day and night. Fix your eyes on Jesus, NOT on
the rubble of the past.

The enemy will try to stir up fear.

Seeing the discouragement, the enemy chose this time to pour a little gas on the flame in the hopes that all of God's work would go up in smoke.

> *And our adversaries said, "They will neither know nor see anything, till we come into their midst and kill them and cause the work to cease." So it was, when the Jews who dwelt near them came, that they told us ten times, "From whatever place you turn, they will be upon us."*
> *Nehemiah 4:11-12*

Fear is a prime weapon of the enemy. He is subtle; he says, "He won't even know that I am inside the wall. I'll finish him off before he ever finishes the job." He used "friends" within the wall to spread rumors about the failure of the work elsewhere and to threaten the servants who were building the wall.

As was the case in Jerusalem, Satan has "friends" who will try to discourage you, too. The rumor mills may begin turning. You will hear that someone you trust supposedly said some terribly negative things about you. You hear of the failure of one of your old friends. You find out that someone you know has cancer. You become discouraged about finances. The enemy will try to pile all of these things on you to discourage you, confuse you and make you afraid. All three of these run counter to faith. When you are sensing discouragement, confusion or fear, then you can be sure that the Lord isn't motivating these thoughts, and this isn't what He has in mind for you. So stop the runaway train of fear and confusion. Focus on Jesus Christ. Read the Word. Sit down with a Christian friend and together you can take the problem to the Lord.

What else can you do to overcome discouragement, confusion and fear? What did the people of Israel do?

> *Therefore I positioned men behind the lower parts of the wall, at the openings; and I set the people according to their families, with their swords, their spears, and their*

bows. And I looked, and arose and said to the nobles, to the leaders, and to the rest of the people, "Do not be afraid of them. Remember the Lord, great and awesome, and fight for your brethren, your sons, your daughters, your wives, and your houses." Nehemiah 4:13-14

First of all, Nehemiah armed the workers. He recognized that danger could come in the midst of the day, that the enemy was likely to attack when the men of Judah were separated along the wall or when they were at home in the night.

How does this apply to us? You are armed for the spiritual battle just as they were armed for a physical one. As a believer in Jesus Christ, the Bible tells us to take up the weapons of spiritual warfare.

For the weapons of our warfare are not carnal but mighty in God for pulling down strongholds, casting down arguments and every high thing that exalts itself against the knowledge of God, bringing every thought into captivity to the obedience of Christ, and being ready to punish all disobedience when your obedience is fulfilled. II Corinthians 10:4-6

Begin the battle by taking thoughts captive. You do not have to entertain or analyze every thought that runs through your mind. Some thoughts, perhaps many thoughts, need to be cast out.

By taking control of your thought-life, you will prevent a lot of anxiety, confusion or discouragement from entering your mind. Think of your thoughts as sheep and goats that are trying to enter the pen. You are the gate-keeper. It is your job to let the sheep in and to keep the goats out. Quickly check each thought to see if it is a lamb – a thought from the Lord, or if it is a goat – a temptation from the enemy or a thought from your sinful past. If it is a lamb, let it in. If it is a goat, shut the door, "The Lord rebuke you, I'm not going to let that thought in my mind."

In addition, you have the whole armor of God described in Ephesians 6:10-17. Verse 11 in that passage says that God gave you the armor so that you can stand against the wiles of the devil. Put on the armor and wear it continually.

There is an ancient story from Ireland that helps to illustrate the importance of wearing the armor of God. Sir John De Courcy was a formidable Norman conqueror who attacked Ireland in the late 12th century and built the castle at Carrickfergus. According to ancient history, he was a strong God-fearing warrior who was captured by a rival knight while kneeling in church. Recognized as a mighty fighter, his rival, Sir Hugh de Lacy knew that he could never defeat De Courcy if he was wearing his armor, and he wore it all of the time, even while he slept. So de Lacy waited until the one time each year when De Courcy took off his armor – on Good Friday when he would kneel before the altar without his shield, harness or weapon. That is when de Lacy attacked with a force of twenty men. De Courcy was a valiant fighter who took thirteen of the men before his cross pole broke. He was taken into captivity and eventually forced into exile.

Sir John De Courcy was invincible as long as he wore his armor. The moral of the story is clear. Put on the full armor of God and wear it every day.

Look at the first advice Nehemiah gave to the people, *"Do not be afraid of them. Remember the Lord, great and awesome, and fight for your brethren, your sons, your daughters, your wives, and your houses."* Do not be afraid of them – remember the Lord! Write this passage on your heart so that you will remember it when the enemy wants to make you afraid. We looked at Romans 8:15 in another chapter, but it is worth repeating here.

> *For you did not receive the spirit of bondage again to fear, but you received the Spirit of adoption by whom we cry out, "Abba, Father." Romans 8:15*

Furthermore …

> *God has not given us a spirit of fear, but of power and of love and of a sound mind. II Timothy 1:7*

God has not given you a spirit of fear. Satan wants to make you afraid, but Jesus wants you to act in faith. Remember Jesus Christ and do not fear the enemy.

"Remember the Lord, great and awesome, and fight for your breth-ren, your sons, your daughters, your wives, and your houses." Fight for your family. Many people will benefit from the work that the Lord is doing in your life – your children, your wife, your parents, neighbors, others. Don't give in to the enemy. Remember that the Lord is involved in this work and it will succeed. And remember that He will use your changed life to change the lives of others, particularly those closest to you.

> *And it happened, when our enemies heard that it was known to us, and that God had brought their plot to noth-ing, that all of us returned to the wall, everyone to his work. Nehemiah 4:15*

The result in Jerusalem was fantastic. The enemies realized that their plan was known and God brought their counsel to nothing. Praise the Lord! The results in your life will be fantastic too. *Submit yourself therefore to God, resist the devil and he will flee from you. Draw near to God and He will draw near to you.* (James 4:7-8a).

Many times, if you will bring the temptations of the enemy into the light, the trouble will roll away like fog that is burned off by the morning sun. How do you bring it to light? Talk with a trustworthy Christian friend and pray together about the problem. Don't settle just for talking about it; be sure to take the temptation to the Lord in prayer.

> *So it was, from that time on, that half of my servants worked at construction, while the other half held the spears, the shields, the bows, and wore armor; and the leaders were behind all the house of Judah. Those who built on the wall, and those who carried burdens, loaded themselves so that with one hand they worked at construc-tion, and with the other held a weapon. Every one of the builders had his sword girded at his side as he built. And the one who sounded the trumpet was beside me. Nehemiah 4:16-18*

The workers labored in one hand with the tools of their trade, and in the other they held a weapon of war. They were protected and they were productive. They were wise enough to know that the enemy could attack at any time – while working, at home, during dinner, etc. So they carried their weapons with them.

Carry your spiritual weapons at all times. Your enemy can attack at any time too. He may tempt you into an argument on the job; he may attempt to draw you into lust during lunch; he can certainly try to make you angry in rush hour traffic on the way home. If you have been leaving Jesus at home when you go out, stop now. You cannot live two separate lives – one as a Christian and the other as someone else. Live every minute as a Spirit-filled believer in Christ Jesus. Carry the sword of the Spirit, the Word of God, everywhere you go. Carry it spiritually by memorizing scripture and praise songs, and pray constantly to the Lord. Carry it physically. Nothing will refresh you in the middle of the day like fifteen minutes with God when all around you seem lost and bound for hell.

I remember working among a crew of lost, hell-bent guys on a construction job years ago. They couldn't draw breath without swearing and threatening to fight each other. It was back-breaking work in the heat of summer. Praying one morning, I felt the Lord direct me to write the title to some praise songs on a piece of paper and stick it in my back pocket. Later that day when the sun was hottest and the language around me was the worst, I pulled out that sheet of paper and began to softly sing one of those songs. Everything changed. The heat was still unbearable; the discussion was as raunchy as ever, but everything inside of me changed. I was strengthened physically and spiritually as I focused my praise on the Lord. The guys working with me even noticed the change in my attitude.

Don't wait for trouble. Develop a plan to win the battle before it begins.

Then I said to the nobles, the rulers, and the rest of the people, "The work is great and extensive, and we are separated far from one another on the wall. "Wherever you hear the sound of the trumpet, rally to us there. Our God will fight for us." So we labored in the work, and half of the men held the spears from daybreak until the stars appeared. At the same time I also said to the people, "Let

173

*each man and his servant stay at night in Jerusalem, that
they may be our guard by night and a working party by
day." So neither I, my brethren, my servants, nor the men of
the guard who followed me took off our clothes, except that
everyone took them off for washing. Nehemiah 4:19-23*

Nehemiah saw the dangers and planned his defenses. An important part of his plan involved cooperation and accountability among the men, whether they were at work or at home. They were accountable to each other, and they maintained contact with each other in order to help defend another man's part of the wall. After this time, the Israelites were constantly on guard, and they supported each other.

Having someone you can call when you are tempted or someone you can pray with daily is a great benefit. The enemy picks off lone sheep like Sanballat's forces tried to pick off lone workers. Don't try to be a lone ranger. Agree to be accountable with someone who can provide Godly counsel and pray with you when you need help. Sometimes the cloud of oppression lifts when we ask a brother to pray with us about an area of weakness where the enemy is attacking.

God did not design the body of Christ to act independently. He created us to act in harmony together, to bear each other's burdens. We strengthen and support each other just as the muscles, nerves, bones, tendons and ligaments in your arm work together to lift weight or shoot a basketball. We are better together, and when we separate ourselves, we are easy prey for the lion that is looking for a lone sheep.

Get involved with a group of healthy Christians. It may be a Sunday School class, a men's discipleship group or a recovery ministry within a local church. If you are a man, find a group of men. If you are a woman, find a group of women. Married couples can work with other married couples, but do not put yourself in a position of sharing your deep spiritual needs with someone of the opposite sex unless you are married to them.

So the frontal attack against Nehemiah and the Israelites ended when the enemy's plans were known, and Nehemiah took wise precautions. When the enemy wages a frontal attack against you, your response should always be the same: submit to the Lord. Resist the devil and he will flee. That is a promise. Draw near to God and He will draw near to you.

Use the tools that God has given in His Word:

- II Corinthians 10:3-5 – take thoughts captive
- Romans 12:1-2 – be transformed as you renew your mind in His Word
- I Corinthians 10:13 – there is a way out of the temptation, look for it and take it
- I Corinthians 6:19-20 – your soul has been purchased with the pure blood of Jesus Christ; therefore, you should honor Him in your body
- John 10:10 – this temptation may look good but the enemy comes in only to kill, steal or destroy; there are long-term consequences to short-term gratification
- Romans 6:22-23 – you are free from sin so you don't have to do it anymore
- Luke 9:23-24 – the world says gratify self; God says if we will deny self then we will find true life, and
- Galatians 6:9 – keep the faith, don't grow weary in well-doing; there are fruitful days ahead!

In chapter 14, we will find out how to win the battle when the enemy tries other means to stop the work that God is doing in your life.

You are involved in a good work!

Possibly for the first time ever, you are actively involved in the good work that Jesus Christ wants to do in your life. And as the old saying goes, "Praise the Lord and pass the ammunition." What kind of ammunition? The spiritual kind.

In chapter 14, you will see the enemies of Israel lobbing salvo after salvo into the city of Jerusalem in efforts to stop the good work that God was doing there. By now, you know that these are the same tactics that your enemy uses to try to stop the good work that Christ is doing in you. Continue mining the Book of Nehemiah, and you will find out how to win the battle against addiction and other sin.

Completing the Good Work
that He has Begun in You

CHAPTER 14

"When we get too comfortable, we set ourselves up to fall. Keep pressing on in the Lord each day. No negotiations, 100% Jesus!"
W.B. – *Beyond Addictions* Graduate 2010

In chapter 13, we looked at three of Satan's most frequently used devices to frustrate the work of God: discouragement, confusion and fear. You are probably on code red alert to be sure that you don't fall into addiction, so your enemy may try to sneak in the back door to discourage or confuse you. He may also attempt to spook you into fear, and tempt you to take his way out of trouble. Then he can cause you to fall. You can defend against these tactics the same way that Nehemiah did, by praying and setting a watch against the enemy day and night. This worked well for the people of Israel, and it will work in your situation too.

What other attack do you need to prepare for?

The distraction of selfishness
As is often the case, the people of Israel were on guard as long as they believed that they were in battle. The trouble came when the battle eased off and they let down their guard.

The enemy could not defeat the Israelites by discouraging them, confusing them or making them run away, but the Israelites almost defeated themselves by their own lust and selfishness. In the fifth chapter of Nehemiah, there is an account of the workers taking advantage of each other rather than looking out for each other's benefit (Nehemiah 5:1-12).

Trials often reveal what is in the heart of a man, and in this time of weakness, the men of Israel tried to exploit each other rather than care for each other. The trouble started with a food shortage in the city and countryside. Some had it and some did not, and the "haves" began to take advantage of the "have nots." It got so bad that those who lacked food had to mortgage their homes and land in order to buy any. When they had no more land, they actually sold their children into slavery in order to put food on the table or pay their taxes. This was taking place among brothers who were supposed to be united against a common enemy. Instead of pulling together to make it through this trial, they began pulling apart and almost succeeded in pulling down the work that God was doing through them.

By human nature we want to serve self first but giving in to the unholy trinity of me, myself and I will frustrate the blessings of God in your life. Mike, a *Beyond Addictions* student, put it this way, "Whenever I've concerned myself with myself for too long, I sense that it saps life out of me. When I'm more into self, God is not welcomed to lead me. Romans 5 says that this separates me from life and peace."

The Bible encourages us to take our eyes off of self and to look out for one another in the body of Christ.

> *Let each of you look out not only for his own interests, but also for the interests of others. Philippians 2:4*

God's Word also says that giving and serving enables us to take our eyes off of our own problems, and it is a great blessing.

> *So let each one give as he purposes in his heart, not grudgingly or of necessity; for God loves a cheerful giver. And God is able to make all grace abound toward you, that you, always having all sufficiency in all things, may have an abundance for every good work. II Corinthians 9:7-8*

You can see from this passage that giving is more an issue of the heart than of the wallet, and this is where the people of Israel were having a problem. It isn't that they were not capable of giving; it was that they were looking at their own desires without considering the needs of others. Then they began to devour each other, and the enemy almost won the battle by waiting for them to destroy themselves. Be on guard. When you are more concerned about your own needs or how you are being served than you are about how you can serve, then you are in trouble. You are harboring lust in your heart, and it will eventually bear bad fruit in your treatment of others.

The passage in I John 3:17 even raises the question of whether you have the love of God in you if you see a brother in need and your heart is not open to help him.

> *But whoever has this world's goods, and sees his brother in need, and shuts up his heart from him, how does the love of God abide in him? I John 3:17*

There is a good Biblical reminder that will guide you as you seek to help your brothers and sisters. We are told in II Thessalonians 3:10 that if a man won't work, neither should he eat, so laziness is no excuse for charity. However, when brothers and sisters are in difficult situations and need our help, we are called upon to provide. In the process, God is glorified. Pray for God's heart for those in need, and remember he who sows bountifully will reap bountifully (II Corinthians 9:6). Someone else's need may be a time for you to sow rather than to reap.

How did Nehemiah respond to the problem? In Nehemiah 5:14-19, you will find that he set the example for giving, and he refused to accept the governor's portion even when it was due him. He did not want to be accused of taking from the poor of Israel that which they needed, and he wanted to be free to give as the Lord directed.

As the governmental leader, he also addressed the problem and required the Israelites to return the people and property to the rightful families and owners. His actions were based upon God's Word.

Deceptive or False Friendships

In chapter 6, the wall is nearing completion. The work is almost done now, right? Not exactly.

> *Now it happened when Sanballat, Tobiah, Geshem the Arab, and the rest of our enemies heard that I had rebuilt the wall, and that there were no breaks left in it (though at that time I had not hung the doors in the gates), that Sanballat and Geshem sent to me, saying, "Come, let us meet together among the villages in the plain of Ono." But they thought to do me harm. So I sent messengers to them, say-*

ing, "I am doing a great work, so that I cannot come down. Why should the work cease while I leave it and go down to you?" Nehemiah 6:1-3

The enemies of Nehemiah encouraged him to drop the work for a few days and take a break. A little vacation could have been mighty tempting. After all, Nehemiah had been serving non-stop for many weeks. Instead of looking for a break, Nehemiah was on guard for a deception, and he saw through the enemy's scheme.

How will the enemy try to draw you out? Will he offer you a free weekend vacation with the guys? Will he tempt you with a date with some foxy mama from your past? Remember, Satan will dangle all kinds of good-looking things before your eyes, but in reality, he seeks nothing but to steal, kill and destroy (John 10:10).

You may hear someone tell you, "Hey, you've been doing well at this Christian thing, the guys really admire you. Come on and go with us to Myrtle Beach for the weekend. We're going to catch some fish, drink a few beers and relax. You need the rest." What should you do? Don't go.

This doesn't mean that it is sinful to take time off for a trip; however, you need to give some serious thought regarding who you are going with and what they are going to be doing.

Nehemiah knew that his enemies weren't interested in blessing him, but in taking him away from the will of God. You can see through the schemes of the enemy too. People will come to you seeming to have your best interest at heart. But do they? The simple test to determine their motive is to check it out with scripture and ask the Holy Spirit to give you discernment. Would Jesus want you to be involved? Why should you leave the great work that the Lord is doing in your life and go back to the world's ways that got you into trouble?

Nehemiah's enemies were persistent. Verse four says that they tried four times to draw him outside of his protection. You have to be just as persistent in your devotion to the Lord. If it was wrong to take them up on the offer the first time, then it is still wrong the fourth time they ask. Stick to your convictions.

False Accusations
When this didn't work, they brought a false accusation that could have ruined the reputation of the work.

180

Then Sanballat sent his servant to me as before, the fifth time, with an open letter in his hand. In it was written: It is reported among the nations, and Geshem says, that you and the Jews plan to rebel; therefore, according to these rumors, you are rebuilding the wall, that you may be their king. And you have also appointed prophets to proclaim concerning you at Jerusalem, saying, 'There is a king in Judah!' Now these matters will be reported to the king. So come, therefore, and let us consult together. Nehemiah 6:5-7

Nehemiah depended upon the good favor of the king, and this kind of report could have brought the work to a screeching halt. But Nehemiah knew that he was right and that their accusation was a lie. What did he do? He answered with a simple, "Not so," and prayed for God to strengthen his hands in the face of this attempt to draw him away.

How should you respond to false accusations? One of the great blessings of your new relationship with Christ is that you do not have to defend your reputation in the face of lies. You will hear false accusations from time to time. Don't worry about them. As long as you are serving Jesus, He provides the defense. God will be your rear guard (Isaiah 52:12 & 58:8). He's got your back. So don't react; respond to God in prayer.

On the other hand, if you are at fault, then confess your sins to Christ and admit your mistake to the ones affected by them. If you are not at fault, let Christ be your defender and just continue doing what He has called you to do.

False Counsel

This time the enemy sent a subtle messenger who appeared Godly but was really a wolf in sheep's clothing.

Afterward I came to the house of Shemaiah the son of Delaiah, the son of Mehetabel, who was a secret informer; and he said, "Let us meet together in the house of God, within the temple, and let us close the doors of the temple, for they are coming to kill you; indeed, at night they will

*come to kill you." And I said, "Should such a man as I flee?
And who is there such as I who would go into the temple to
save his life? I will not go in!" Then I perceived that God
had not sent him at all, but that he pronounced this prophecy against me because Tobiah and Sanballat had hired him.
For this reason he was hired, that I should be afraid and
act that way and sin, so that they might have cause for an
evil report, that they might reproach me. My God, remember Tobiah and Sanballat, according to these their works,
and the prophetess Noadiah and the rest of the prophets
who would have made me afraid.
Nehemiah 6:10-14*

The enemy had hired the priest! How did Nehemiah know that the counsel of the priest was not from the Lord?

First of all, his advice was against God's law. He was encouraging Nehemiah to hide in the Holy Place of the Temple. Nehemiah was not a priest and he wasn't supposed to go into the Holy Place. If Nehemiah had listened, he would have brought a reproach on the work by clearly disobeying the commandments of God. You can imagine how the peo-ple would have responded to this, "Can you believe that Nehemiah broke the commandment to go into the Holy Place? He's not a priest. And he did this all because he was afraid of good old Sanballat." They would have lost respect for their leader, and the enemy would have had a field day spreading gossip about his actions.

Thank God that Nehemiah knew the Word. That is how he knew that the priest's counsel was ungodly even though it came from some-one who was supposed to represent God.

Like Nehemiah, you need to be careful who you receive counsel from. Just because someone wears a cross or quotes scripture, that doesn't mean that they are walking with the Lord. Be sure to find God-ly counselors that you can trust. Be like the Bereans in Acts 17:11.

*These were more fair-minded than those in Thessalonica,
in that they received the word with all readiness, and
searched the Scriptures daily to find out whether these things
were so. Acts 17:11*

The people of Berea listened to Paul preach, but they took personal responsibility for finding out if he was teaching the truth. You are I are called to take the same responsibility. Make sure that you are being taught the truth. Study the Word of God yourself, and you will know if "these things are so."

Secondly, Shemaiah the priest also tried to use fear to motivate Nehemiah. We have already addressed this issue, but remember Romans 8:15 says that *you have not received the spirit of bondage again to fear; but you have received the Spirit of adoption, whereby we cry, Abba, Father.* If fear is the driving force, then the motive for taking an action is probably not from God. When we act out of fear, we are not responding in faith. Instead of fearing, cry out to your Heavenly Father.

Lastly, when receiving counsel, remember Colossians 3:15 and let the peace of God rule or umpire in your heart. Ask the following questions when you are receiving counsel. Do you have a sense of peace about the advice that you are given? Does it ring true with the Word of God? Is the person counseling you trying to motivate you with fear? The answers to these questions will help you determine if the advice is Godly or not.

It is finished!

So the wall was finished on the twenty-fifth day of Elul, in fifty-two days. And it happened, when all our enemies heard of it, and all the nations around us saw these things, that they were very disheartened in their own eyes; for they perceived that this work was done by our God. Nehemiah 6:15-16

The wall of protection is finished. The people of Israel were recognized as a strong, united people with a strong wall. They no longer had to worry about bands of marauders coming in and stealing their goods or harming their children. The enemies of Israel *"were very disheartened in their own eyes, for they perceived that this work was done by our God."* Amen and amen!

We come to the point where we began two chapters ago when we said that the work would speak for itself. Once people begin to see that God is doing the work in your life, their response to you will change too. Some will be encouraged; others will be discouraged, and for a while they will give up trying to draw you away. You are safe as you abide in Christ.

You have committed to building a good foundation in your life. Praise the Lord for your good beginning! However, you still need to beware of one more issue ...

Compromise

> *Also in those days the nobles of Judah sent many let-ters to Tobiah, and the letters of Tobiah came to them. For many in Judah were pledged to him, because he was the son-in-law of Shechaniah the son of Arah, and his son Je-hohanan had married the daughter of Meshullam the son of Berechiah. Also they reported his good deeds before me, and reported my words to him. Tobiah sent letters to fright-en me. Nehemiah 6:17-19*

In Nehemiah's case, there were men within the walls who were al-lies of Tobiah. They maintained communication with this enemy and sought to convince Nehemiah that good old Tobiah wasn't such a bad guy after all. They also repeated to Tobiah conversations they had with Nehemiah.

The people of Israel were compromising with the same enemy who had tried to kill them. How could they do such a thing? They probably drifted slowly into compromise. This trick of the devil kills inch by inch, and there is no place for it when you are confronted with tempta-tion.

Satan, your enemy, will attempt to draw you away little by little. He knows that it isn't likely for you to fall into drug use or drunkenness overnight, and he is aware that your defense system is on alert for a frontal attack. So how will he try to get you back into his net? He may tempt you with an alluring woman or man who leads you away from God. He or she looks good and righteous on your first or second meet-ing, but the longer you know them the more you realize that they aren't the good Christian that they appeared to be. Your affection for them may tempt you away from your love for Christ, and before you realize it, you are living in sin and dealing with the consequences.

Satan may also tempt you into compromise at work or in social situations where you are overly concerned with the opinions of unbelievers around you. "One drink won't hurt. I've got to fit in or I may lose my job." And it may not hurt … yet. You will be led further into the trap until you drink two or three beers or split a bag of marijuana with your old buddies, and then you will be back in trouble.

Some time after the events of chapter six, Nehemiah left the city to return to the king's palace at Shushan. During his absence, the enemy moved in slowly until he had taken up residence in the Temple. When Nehemiah returned to Jerusalem, he was grieved by what he saw, but he also knew how to handle the problem.

> *But during all this I was not in Jerusalem, for in the thirty-second year of Artaxerxes king of Babylon I had returned to the king. Then after certain days I obtained leave from the king, and I came to Jerusalem and discovered the evil that Eliashib had done for Tobiah, in preparing a room for him in the courts of the house of God. And it grieved me bitterly; therefore I threw all the household goods of Tobiah out of the room. Then I commanded them to cleanse the rooms; and I brought back into them the articles of the house of God, with the grain offering and the frankincense. Nehemiah 13:6-9*

During Nehemiah's absence, a great deal of corruption had taken place. They actually removed the articles of worship from a storage room in the Temple and set up a little efficiency apartment for Tobiah, one of the enemies who had tried years before to destroy them.

This is unbelievable! How could they forget? How could they compromise their worship of God in order to appease their enemy? We would never do anything like that, would we?

Have you ever seen a Christian brother who was sold out for Jesus one year, and by the next, he was inviting you to his house for a keg party? Or maybe he begins emailing you dirty jokes, and you wonder what happened to him. He may still claim to have a relationship with Jesus, but Jesus no longer rules in his heart. Instead, he has converted the place that Jesus once occupied into a room for his own pleasure.

Over time, compromise has eroded his devotion to Jesus, and he is at risk of falling back into a sinful lifestyle.

How can you avoid this problem? It's really pretty simple. You can be free from the problems of compromise the same way that Nehemiah set the people of Jerusalem free. He cleaned house. He threw Tobiah's stuff out and put the articles of worship back where they belonged. Do a little heart cleaning and find out what you may be harboring there too. Remember King David's prayer in Psalm 139. It's a great heart cleanser.

> *Search me, O God, and know my heart; Try me, and know my anxieties; and see if there is any wicked way in me, and lead me in the way everlasting. Psalm 139:23-24*

So be it.

Nehemiah also had to address some other issues of compromise that had seeped into Jerusalem. Nehemiah chapter 13 details the steps that he took to root out all of the corruption that occurred during his absence.

- The Israelites had been breaking the Sabbath law set down by God for the Jews. They were working, buying and selling on the Sabbath in direct violation of God's commandment. They must have forgotten that their failure to observe the Jewish Sabbath was one of the reasons that God sent them into captivity, but alas, people's memories are short. It is important to remember where your own sins have led. You don't want to live in the past, but it is healthy to recall that satisfying that little desire of the flesh led you deeper into addiction, and it cost more than you ever wanted to pay. Don't go back.

- In verses 23-28, Nehemiah discovered that the Israelites had been intermarrying with those of other beliefs. One of the priest's sons had married the daughter of Sanballat. God warns us not to be unequally yoked with unbelievers, for what fellowship has righteousness with lawlessness? And what communion has light with darkness? (II Corinthians 6:14) Being "unequally yoked" covers a lot of territory, i.e., possible marriage partners, business partners, close friends, etc. The bottom line is not to be brought into partnership with unbelievers. If you do, then you will be open to compromising your faith. *Do not be deceived: Evil company corrupts good habits* (I Corinthians 15:33).

Beware of compromise in your new life.

Virtually all of the trouble experienced by the Israelites once the wall was built can be attributed to compromise in their relationship with God. The same is true for us. You are in good shape right now. The Lord has cleansed you from the inside out. You are closer to Him than you have been in a long time. Your thoughts are clearer, your mind is sharper.

All you need to do is to continue walking in the Spirit. Remember:

As you have therefore received Christ Jesus the Lord, so walk in Him, rooted and built up in Him and established in the faith, as you have been taught, abounding in it with thanksgiving. Colossians 2:6-7

Think about the lessons in this discipleship study and continue walking this path of life as the Holy Spirit directs you.

- You are being transformed as you renew your mind in the Word of God.
- You have a fresh view of who God is, of His sufficiency for you and your identity in His Son Jesus Christ.
- You now understand that addiction is a form of idolatry that interferes with your relationship with the Lord.
- You have found Biblical counsel for problems related to pride, anger, self-discipline and personal relationships.
- You have allowed the Lord to cleanse your body (the temple of the Holy Spirit) and begun to build a wall around your thought-life and behavior as a new creation in Christ.

Protect it. Diligently keep the wall, and do not permit the enemy to creep in through compromise. Be careful what you permit in your life through the TV, in the music you listen to, in your close relationships, and in the places you go. They may appear innocent on the front end, but sin practiced over and over will cause you to compromise your relationship with Jesus, and rob you of the blessings that He gives.

Remember, Jesus is the one who came in order that you might have abundant life; Satan and his little demons want to steal from you, kill you, and destroy you. Don't compromise with him.

The best way to avoid compromise is to be separated unto Jesus Christ. It can be difficult to figure out how to be separated from all of the sin that swirls around you. The best way that I have found is to draw closer to Jesus Christ. If you are with Him every day, seeking Him through prayer, meditation and reading His Word, then you will be free from the issues that the enemy would use to hold you in bondage to your past.

> *And do this, knowing the time, that now it is high time to awake out of sleep; for now our salvation is nearer than when we first believed. The night is far spent, the day is at hand. Therefore let us cast off the works of darkness, and let us put on the armor of light. Let us walk properly, as in the day, not in revelry and drunkenness, not in lewdness and lust, not in strife and envy. But put on the Lord Jesus Christ, and make no provision for the flesh, to fulfill its lusts. Romans 13:11-14*

The best way to cast off the works of darkness is to put on the armor of light, to put on the Lord Jesus Christ. This is how Nehemiah taught the Israelites to win the battle. It wasn't by constantly fearing their enemies or even by understanding all of their tactics, it was by remaining secure inside the walls of the city. We are victorious as we put on the Lord Jesus Christ, our armor of light. We remain secure as long as we abide in Him.

Conclusion

Through the last three chapters, we have looked at Nehemiah's commitment to the Lord and the incredible way that he led the people of Israel to rebuild the massive walls around the city of Jerusalem. As we close, put yourself in the place of the people who were living there before he came and worked to rebuild the wall. They lived in constant fear of the enemy outside who seemed friendly one minute and stole from them the next. They had no security and no hope for anything better. Then Nehemiah arrived on the scene. He told them the good news of why he came – to give them freedom and security. Throughout the project, they succeeded as long as they kept their eyes on their leader and followed his direction. Even though there were difficult trials, they still succeeded because they followed the words and the example of Nehemiah.

You probably see the parallel between their situation and yours. You were living in fear, confusion and discouragement before Jesus entered your life. He came bearing good news – He came to set you free and to give you assurance for the future. As long as you keep your eyes on Him and follow His direction, then you succeed, even through the storms and trials of this life. Maintain a daily commitment to walk with Him. Don't allow the enemy to whisper his deceptive, compromising thoughts into your ear. If you do these things, you will enjoy living in the presence of God, and you will remain free from addiction.

Be free. The cords of sin do not have to hold you down any longer. Jesus Christ has set you free by His own blood, and He sent the Holy Spirit to live in you, and to lead you into continuous freedom from sin.

Victory!

Putting It All to Work

Chapter 15

If then the son makes you free, you will be truly free.
John 8:36 (Bible in Basic English)

What is the secret to continuous freedom? It is surrender to the will of God. The Bible teaches you that you can trust Jesus Christ. In this book, we have applied more than 200 scripture passages that enable you to move beyond addiction. Jesus loves you, and He wants you to live victoriously as you abide in Him.

You have learned a lot about addiction and being free from it. There is a warning and a promise in the first chapter of the Book of James that you need to remember.

> *Therefore lay aside all filthiness and overflow of wickedness, and receive with meekness the implanted word, which is able to save your souls. <u>But be doers of the word, and not hearers only, deceiving yourselves</u>. For if anyone is a hearer of the word and not a doer, he is like a man observing his natural face in a mirror; for he observes himself, goes away, and immediately forgets what kind of man he was. But he who looks into the perfect law of liberty and continues in it, and is not a forgetful hearer but a doer of the work, this one will be blessed in what he does. James 1:21-25*

The man who reads the Word or just hears the Word without applying it is like a man who looks at himself in the mirror, sees his dirty face that needs a shave, and walks away without doing anything about it. That man is self-deceived. He believes that he is alright because he has knowledge of what he should do to fix the problem but he still has the problem. On the other hand, the man who continues in the Word and applies it will be blessed in what he does. Simply put, apply the lessons that you have learned. Do not be content to read them; put them to work and you will be blessed.

Remember the blessed truth of regeneration – being born again by the Spirit of God. If you are a Christian, you are a new creation in Christ. Old things have passed away, and all things have become new (II Corinthians 5:17). This may be an understatement of the quality of new life you have in Jesus Christ. Having been set free from the sinful addictions that robbed you of life, you are now free to pursue the life of freedom that you have in Him. Remember Augustine's response when sin came calling, "I know that it is you but it's not me." He was no longer the same old man who would fall to temptation; he was a new man in Christ Jesus. So are you.

You are free.

> *If the Son therefore shall make you free, you shall be free indeed! John 8:36*

Be separated unto Jesus Christ; draw close to Him each day just as you would draw near to a loving father when danger is near. By surrendering to His direction, you will avoid the sins of the past and be free from danger.

God's Word promises us in Galatians 5:16 that if we walk in the Spirit, we will not fulfill the desires of the flesh. It does not say that we *might* not fulfill the desires of the flesh; it says that we *will* not do it. Walking in the Spirit guarantees our freedom from sin. The choice is ours. Like Joshua said, *I don't know what choice you will make but as for me and my house, we will serve the Lord (Joshua 24:15).* I pray that you choose the same.

Hebrews 12:1-2 sums up the *Beyond Addictions* message as well as anything. Study it. Put it to work in your life and may the Lord bless you.

> *Therefore we also, since we are surrounded by so great a cloud of witnesses, let us lay aside every weight, and the sin which so easily ensnares us, and let us run with endurance the race that is set before us, looking unto Jesus, the author and finisher of our faith, who for the joy that was set before Him endured the cross, despising the shame,*

and has sat down at the right hand of the throne of God.
Hebrews 12:1-2

Get involved in a good, Bible-teaching church. Spend time with healthy Christians who are walking with Jesus.

Do not be content to learn the principles of being free in Christ. Live the life!

APPENDIX A
FOUNDATIONAL VERSES FOR BEYOND ADDICTIONS

1. You are a new creation.
Therefore, if anyone is in Christ, he is a new creation; old things have passed away; behold, all things have become new. II Corinthians 5:17

2. Transform your mind.
I beseech you therefore, brethren, by the mercies of God, that you present your bodies a living sacrifice, holy, acceptable to God, which is your reasonable service. And do not be conformed to this world, but be transformed by the renewing of your mind, that you may prove what is that good and acceptable and perfect will of God. Romans 12:1-2

3. By giving us Himself, God has given us all that we need.
As His divine power has given to us all things that pertain to life and godliness, through the knowledge of Him who called us by glory and virtue. II Peter 1:3

4. You can take thoughts captive.
For though we walk in the flesh, we do not war according to the flesh. For the weapons of our warfare are not carnal but mighty in God for pulling down strongholds, casting down arguments and every high thing that exalts itself against the knowledge of God, bringing every thought into captivity to the obedience of Christ. II Corinthians 10:3-5

5. You have abundant life in Christ.
The thief does not come except to steal, and to kill, and to destroy. I have come that they may have life, and that they may have it more abundantly. John 10:10

6. We are under new management.
Or do you not know that your body is the temple of the Holy Spirit who is in you, whom you have from God, and you are not your own? For you were bought at a price; therefore glorify God in your body and in your spirit, which are God's. I Corinthians 6:19-20

7. Win the fight against   temptation.
No temptation has overtaken you except such as is common to man; but God is faithful, who will not allow you to be tempted beyond what you are able, but with the temptation will also make the way of escape, that you may be able to bear it. I Corinthians 10:13

8. You can guard your heart against lust.
But each one is tempted when he is drawn away by his own desires and

enticed. Then, when desire has conceived, it gives birth to sin; and sin, when it is full-grown, brings forth death. James 1:14-15

9. God is thinking about you.

For I know the thoughts that I think toward you, says the LORD, thoughts of peace and not of evil, to give you a future and a hope. Jeremiah 29:11

10. God is looking for men with perfect hearts.

For the eyes of the LORD run to and fro throughout the whole earth, to show Himself strong on behalf of those whose heart is loyal to Him. II Chronicles 16:9a

11. We are free from sin through Jesus Christ.

But now having been set free from sin, and having become slaves of God, you have your fruit to holiness, and the end, everlasting life. For the wages of sin is death, but the gift of God is eternal life in Christ Jesus our Lord. Romans 6:22-23

12. When you deny self you will find true life.

Then He said to them all, "If anyone desires to come after Me, let him deny himself, and take up his cross daily, and follow Me. For whoever desires to save his life will lose it, but whoever loses his life for My sake will save it. Luke 9:23-24

13. Be doers of the Word.

Therefore lay aside all filthiness and overflow of wickedness, and receive with meekness the implanted word, which is able to save your souls. But be doers of the word, and not hearers only, deceiving yourselves. James 1:21-22

14. Study God's Word.

Be diligent to present yourself approved to God, a worker who does not need to be ashamed, rightly dividing the word of truth. II Timothy 2:15

15. Remember, Jesus is our Wonderful Counselor.

For unto us a Child is born, Unto us a Son is given; And the government will be upon His shoulder. And His name will be called Wonderful, Counselor, Mighty God, Everlasting Father, Prince of Peace. Isaiah 9:6

16. Keep the faith until the end.

And let us not grow weary while doing good, for in due season we shall reap if we do not lose heart. Galatians 6:9

APPENDIX B
SCRIPTURE REFERENCES

Listed in order of use in each chapter.
Chapter 1 – Beginning at the Beginning
II Corinthians 5:17
I Corinthians 10:13
Isaiah 53:6
Ephesians 2:10
Jeremiah 29:11

Chapter 2 - Transforming the Way We Think
Romans 12:1-2
James 1:14-15
Ephesians 5:25-26
II Corinthians 3:18
Hebrews 4:12
II Timothy 3:16-17
John 14:16-17, 26
Romans 15:14
II Corinthians 1:3-4

Chapter 3 – How Did We Descend Into Addiction?
Proverbs 9:13-18
James 1:14
Proverbs 23:35
Judges 14:1-3
Judges 14:5-7
Judges 14:8-9
Judges 16:1
Judges 16:4
Judges 16:20-21
Hebrews 12:1-2

Chapter 4 – Addiction as Idolatry
I John 5:20-21
Ezekiel 14:3
I Corinthians 10:6-12
I Corinthians 10:13
I Corinthians 10:14
Ephesians 5:5

Colossians 3:5
II Corinthians 10:3-5
James 4:7-8
Luke 4:1-13
Ephesians 6:12-18
Philippians 4:8
II Corinthians 6:16-17
Psalm 139:23-24

Chapter 5 – Other Biblical Views of Addiction
Psalm 45:7
John 8:34
James 1:12-15
Galatians 5:1
Jeremiah 3:8-9
Ezekiel 23:37
Proverbs 7:1-5
Proverbs 7:6-15
Proverbs 7:21-23
Proverbs 7:24-27
Isaiah 53:5-6

Chapter 6 – That I May Know Him
Philippians 3:8-11, 13-14
John 17:3
John 10:10
Exodus 3:13-14
Genesis 22:13-14
Exodus 15:26
Exodus 17:8-15
Judges 6:24
Jeremiah 23:6
Ezekiel 48:35
Psalm 91:1-4, 14-16
Exodus 34:6-7
Romans 5:8
Deuteronomy 5:9
I John 1:7,9
II Corinthians 4:6
John 14:9
John 6:48
John 8:12

John 10:9, 11
John 11:25
John 14:6
John 15:1
Matthew 11:28-30
Philippians 2:5-8

Chapter 7 – Jesus Christ is Sufficient for All Things
Colossians 1:16
Revelation 4:11
Colossians 1:19
Colossians 2:3-4
Colossians 2:6-7, 8, 9-10
Psalm 23:1-3
Luke 4:18-21
Colossians 1:13
John 4:13-14
II Peter 2:1-3
Isaiah 9:6
Psalm 32:8-9
II Corinthians 11:3
Isaiah 26:3
II Corinthians 1:8-10
II Corinthians 3:4-5
John 15:5
II Corinthians 4:6-7

Chapter 8 – Your New Identity in Christ
II Corinthians 5:17
Psalm 103:12
Ephesians 1:3-5
I Peter 2:9
Romans 8:14-15
Ephesians 1:7
Romans 3:23-24
Romans 5:8
Ephesians 2:5-7
Ephesians 2:10
Colossians 2:9-10
II Peter 1:3
Romans 13:13-14
Galatians 2:20

Chapter 9 – Making the Change
II Corinthians 5:17

Chapter 10 – Godly Wisdom for Pride and Anger
Proverbs 29:23
Proverbs 6:16-19
Proverbs 16:5
Isaiah 14:12-15
Proverbs 29:23
II Corinthians 3:18
Matthew 10:39
Proverbs 15:25
Proverbs 18:12
Proverbs 16:18
Proverbs 3:7
Proverbs 12:15
Proverbs 10:8
Proverbs 13:10
Proverbs 21:24
Proverbs 8:13
Proverbs 3:34
Proverbs 13:10
Proverbs 28:25
Proverbs 29:22
James 3:14-16
James 4:1
Proverbs 14:29, 16
Proverbs 25:28
Proverbs 16:32
Proverbs 20:22
Romans 12:17-19
Luke 15:28-32
Proverbs 15:18
Colossians 3:8
Ephesians 4:31
Galatians 5:22-23
Proverbs 10:12
I John 1:7-9
Ephesians 4:32

Chapter 11 – Godly Wisdom for Self-discipline and Developing Friendships

Hebrews 6:11-15
Hebrews 10:35-37
II Peter 3:14-15
Proverbs 10:4
Proverbs 22:29
Proverbs 6:6-11
Proverbs 24:30-34
Proverbs 10:26
Ecclesiastes 10:18
Proverbs 15:19
Proverbs 13:4
Colossians 3:22-25
Ecclesiastes 4:9-12
James 4:4
I John 2:15-17
Proverbs 18:24
Proverbs 13:20
Proverbs 12:26
Proverbs 16:28-29
Proverbs 22:24-25
I Corinthians 15:33
II Corinthians 6:14
Matthew 19:4-6

Chapter 12 – The Eternal Construction Project

Nehemiah 2:11
Colossians 2:6-7
Nehemiah 1:1-4
James 4:5-7
Nehemiah 2:9, 10
John 16:33
Nehemiah 2:17-18
II Chronicles 16:9
Nehemiah 2:19-20
Colossians 2:9-10

Chapter 13 – Continuing the Work of Jesus Christ

Nehemiah 4:1-3
Nehemiah 4:4-6
Hebrews 10:35-36

Nehemiah 4:7-9, 10
Psalm 1:1-2
Nehemiah 4:11-12, 13-14
II Corinthians 10:4-6
Romans 8:15
II Timothy 1:7
Nehemiah 4:15, 16-18, 19-23

Chapter 14 – Completing the Good Work that He Has Begun in You
Ephesians 5:8
Nehemiah 5:1-12
Philippians 2:4
II Corinthians 9:7-8
I John 3:17
Nehemiah 6:1-3
Nehemiah 6:5-7
Nehemiah 6:10-14
Acts 17:11
Nehemiah 6:15-16, 17-19
Nehemiah 13:6-9
Psalm 139:23-24
Colossians 2:6-7
Romans 13:11-14

Chapter 15 – Putting it All to Work
John 8:36
James 1:21-25
Hebrews 12:1-2

APPENDIX C
ASSIGNMENTS FOR THE BEYOND ADDICTIONS COURSE

Changing the way we think:

Being transformed by the renewing of our minds.

Lessons 1 & 2

(Chapters 1 & 2)

Name: _____

Have you ever been through a rehabilitation program? As you can see in chapter one, God offers us something deeper and more effective. He offers transformation. What is the difference between rehabilitation and transformation? _____

_____

_____

_____

_____

1. Are you are still actively engaged in sinful addictions? Do you still think about it on a regular basis? If so, you are still going the wrong way. Romans 12:1-2 tells you how to turn things around. Write this passage here: _____

_____

_____

_____

2. Are you engaged in any activities that might cause you to be shaped by the thinking of this world (through movies or programs, books or magazines, music or programs you listen to, ungodly counsel you receive)? _____

_____

_____

_____

3. Romans 12:2 tells us what we should do instead of being shaped by the influences of the world. It says that we should be transformed by renewing our mind. How can you start the process of renewing or renovating your mind this week?

_____

_____

_____

_____

Write down an action that you can take today to start this process.

_____

_____

4. James 1:14-15 tells us that everyone faces temptation. Who is the tempter and what can we do about him? _____

_____

_____

_____

5. The call to resist temptation and to be transformed by the renewal of your mind is tough. Did Jesus Christ leave you to live this life on your own? _____

If not, then who did He send and how does He help you? (Hint: consider what you are taught by John 14:16 & 14:26)

_____

_____

_____

_____

6. Read Hebrews 4:12 and II Timothy 3:16-17. In your own words, tell me what these verses mean to you as you fight the battle against addiction? _____

_____

_____

_____

_____

_____

Notes:

How did we descend into addiction?

Lesson 3

Name: _____

1. Do you agree with Dr. Welch's definition of addiction? _____

2. If so, what substances, activities or state of mind have held you captive in the past?_____

_____

_____

_____

3. Write James 1:14 here: _____

_____

_____

Are you harboring any lust in your heart that Satan the fisherman could use to entice you? _____ If so (and you probably are), what can you do about it?

_____

_____

_____

4. Was there a time in your past when the following statement was true in your life? If so, when was it? "Drawn away by our own lust, we were ripe for the picking. At the time, we didn't know that we were descending into an addiction ... We thought we were flying high above the clouds but we were really descending to a banquet in the grave. Later when our eyes opened we were horrified to see that it was filled with dead men's bones. The thing that we used for our

pleasure began to use us." _____

_____

_____

_____

5. When Jesus met the woman at the well in the fourth chapter of the
   Book of John, He pointed to one solution to her problem. Who or
   what was it? _____ Like the woman in
   John 4, you have been drinking from the wrong wells too. Where can
   you find the solution to your problem? _____

_____

_____

Write down an action that you can take today to start this process.

_____

_____

_____

6. Samson's troubles began when he went down to Timnah. Was there a
   time when you "went down to Timnah" too? _____ What was this
   simple step into sin that led you into further addiction?

_____

_____

_____

7. Samson was a very gifted man. Why did he experience so many problems with temptation and sin? _____

_____

_____

8. Are there any old "carcasses" in your past that could tempt you?

   _____

   What should you do to avoid going back to see if there is any sweetness left in them?

   _____

   _____

   _____

9. Read II Corinthians 5:17 and tell me how this passage can help you
   steer clear from old temptations that Satan may want to use to entice
   you back into a life of sin. _____

   _____

   _____

10. How can you apply Hebrews 12:1-2 today to help you stay away from
    previous sins that so easily entangled you?

    _____

    _____

    _____

11. What is the most meaningful thing you learned from this lesson?

    _____

    _____

    _____

    _____

Addiction as Idolatry

Lesson 4

Name: _____

1. After reading this lesson, do you think that you have ever purchased an idol from a vendor on the street? _____ Can you identify any idols in your past that you looked to for something that you thought God could not provide? _____ What were they? _____

_____

_____

_____

2. What is an idol? (Re-read pages 1-2 in the lesson.)

_____

_____

_____

_____

3. Dr. Edward Welch says, "Idolatry includes anything we worship: the lust for pleasure, respect, love, power, control, or freedom from pain. … The problem is not the idolatrous substance; it is the false worship of the heart." Can you identify any idolatrous thoughts that you may still be worshipping in your heart and mind? _____ If so, what are they? _____

_____

_____

_____

4. In I Corinthians 10:6-14, Paul lists four examples of failure that resulted from idolatry when the Israelites were traveling through the wilderness. Briefly list those four examples:

   1) _____

   2)_____

   3)_____

   4)_____

5. Paul concludes his statement in I Corinthians 10:6-14 by saying, "Therefore, let him who thinks he stands take heed lest he fall." How can you take Paul's warning to heart as you look at the four ways that the Israelites failed in the wilderness? _____

   _____

   _____

   _____

6. The Bible continuously warns us against covetousness and lust. Does the Bible really consider those sinful desires to be idolatry? _____ How can a little dissatisfaction with circumstances in your life can lead to idolatry?

   _____

   _____

   _____

   _____

7. Tell me how you can avoid this problem of coveting and idolatry._____

_____

_____

_____

_____

8. As you pray Psalm 139:23-24, are there any specific thoughts that
    you believe the Lord is asking you to bring into subjection to Him?
    _____ If so, keep giving them up to the Lord. Confess weakness
    in this area of your life and ask the Holy Spirit for help in overcoming
    these problems.

9. What is the most meaningful thing you learned from this lesson?

    _____

_____

_____

_____

_____

Notes:

Other Biblical Views of Addiction

Lesson 5

Name: _____

1. This lesson begins with the story of a man named Jim who was asking the Lord to remove a sinful habit from his life but still secretly loved the habit. Are there any addictions in your life that you have asked God to remove but are still secretly enjoying? _____. What should you do about them?

    _____

    _____

    _____

2. How can an addiction be considered "voluntary slavery"?

    _____

    _____

    _____

Are there any scripture passages from the lesson that help to explain it in this light? _____

_____

3. Read John 8:36 and tell me how this solves the problem created by John 8:34 _____

    _____

    _____

4. How can a sinful attachment to something be considered an act of spiritual adultery against the Lord? _____

_____

_____

_____

5. The lesson includes a long passage from Proverbs 7. Read Proverbs 7:1-5 and tell me how applying God's Word can protect you from someone or something that wants to flatter you into doing something that you know you should not do. _____

_____

_____

6. Finish this statement: "You will never receive true happiness through _____".

7. Define "unrighteousness". _____

_____

_____

_____

8. What does the book *Self Confrontation: A Manual for In-Depth Biblical Discipleship* call addictions?

_____

Review the list on pgs. 64-65 in the lesson and tell me if you are currently engaged in any habits that fit four or more of the descriptions in this list of thirteen characteristics. _____

_____

9. How does Isaiah 53:5-6 provide a solution to this problem of life-dominating sin? _____

_____

_____

10. Read the five foundational scriptures at the end of the lesson. Which of these is most meaningful to you at this point?

_____

Why? _____

_____

_____

_____

Notes:

That I May Know Him

✤Lesson 6

Name: _____

1. "That I may know Him". In these words, the Apostle Paul expressed the focus of his life, that he might know Jesus. On a scale of 1-100, how close would you say you come to having the same desire (1 being not very close and 100 being the same as Paul)? _____ How does this desire affect your struggle with addiction? _____

_____

_____

2. According to this lesson, why were Adam and Eve created?

_____

Why did Jesus pay the price to redeem you and me? _____

_____

3. This chapter includes six "I Am" statements from the Old Testament. Each one tells you something about God. Which is the most important to you right now? _____.

Why? _____

_____

4. You have probably heard about God Almighty. In this lesson, you find out what that really means. What are the two meanings of El Shaddai or God Almighty? 1) _____

and 2) _____.

5. In which of these two ways do you see God most?

_____.

Why? _____

_____

_____

6. What does the name of Jesus mean?

_____

Jesus made seven "I Am" statements in the Book of John. Which of these

means the most to you? _____ Why?

_____

_____

_____

7. Read Matthew 11:28-30. Have you searched for peace in your life?
   How does this passage reassure you that you do not need to look anywhere other than Jesus to find the rest and peace that you have desired? _____

_____

_____

8. What is wrong with this statement? "I can't come to Jesus until I get
   cleaned up." _____

_____

_____

9. What did you learn about the nature of Jesus in this lesson?

_____

_____

_____

_____

10. How does growing closer to Jesus keep you free from addiction?

_____

_____

_____

_____

Notes:

Jesus Christ is All Sufficient

Lesson 7

Name: _____

1. "People without a relationship with their personal Creator are hunger-
    ing for happiness, meaning and fulfillment but nothing this planet of-
    fers can fully satisfy these longings," says Kenneth Boa. How does
    this describe your experiences before you met Jesus?

    _____

    _____

    _____

2. According to the lesson, how can you triumph over sin and remove
    addictions from your life? _____

    _____

    _____

3. Colossians 1:16 has some interesting things to say about Jesus. Ac-
    cording to this passage, why was the earth and everything in it creat-
    ed? _____

Read Revelation 4:11 too. These two passages help us understand the purpose
God had in creating you. What is it?

_____

_____

4. What does it mean to you to know that all fullness is found in Jesus
    Christ? _____

_____

5. What did Paul mean when he said that "my God shall supply all my needs according to His riches in glory"? _____

_____

_____

6. Compare the satisfaction that Jesus gives to what you experienced before you knew Him. _____

_____

_____

_____

7. It is important to receive counsel from God. How does God counsel you? _____

_____

_____

8. John 15:5 says a mouthful. What do you think it means to abide in Jesus? _____

_____

_____

_____

How does abiding in Jesus compare to visiting Him once or twice a week in church? _____

_____

9. What did Paul mean when he said, "Not that we are sufficient of ourselves to think of anything as being from ourselves, but our sufficiency is from God" (II Corinthians 3:4-5)? _____

_____

_____

10. Please tell me how knowing that Jesus is sufficient for all things can help to free you from addictions. _____

_____

_____

_____

_____

_____

Notes:

Your new Identity in Christ

Lessons 8 & 9

(Chapters 8 & 9)

Name: _____

1. According to A.W. Tozer, why did Jesus suffer and
   die?_____

How does this enable you to part from your old sinful nature?

_____

_____

_____

2. Re-read the portion of the lesson that deals with your adoption into
   the family of God. What does this mean to you?

_____

_____

_____

_____

Can you relate to the struggles of the Russian orphans who were adopted by
their American parents? _____ If so, how do you relate?

_____

_____

3. What does it mean to be dead to sin?

_____

_____

4. As a Christian, you are complete in Christ. Where did you try to find fulfillment in the past?

_____

_____

Practically, what does it mean to know that you are now complete in Christ?

_____

_____

_____

_____

_____

5. How do you apply II Corinthians 5:17 to your life? _____

_____

_____

_____

6. The Bible says a lot about you as a believer in Jesus. Which of the descriptions are most important to you? _____

_____

_____

_____

7. Making the Change – How has your understanding of addiction changed since you started the class? _____

_____

_____

_____

_____

8. How has your relationship with Jesus changed since you started the class? _____

_____

_____

_____

_____

Notes:

Godly Wisdom for Pride and Anger

Lesson 10

1. How is pride referred to in the book of Proverbs?

   _____

Have you ever been in a treatment program or class that referred to it this way? _____

2. Re-read the three passages from Proverbs and tell me what pride leads to._____

   _____

   _____

   _____

3. How does pride interfere with your ability to learn and to grow?

   _____

   _____

   _____

4. How does pride cause bitterness and contention? _____

   _____

   _____

   _____

5. The Bible has a lot to say about humility. How would you describe this Biblical virtue?_____

   _____

_____

_____

6. How is a man without self-control like a city without walls?

    _____

    _____

    _____

7. Can you relate to the older brother who became angry when the father poured out his blessing on the younger brother? _____ How did you respond the last time that someone got a job or a promotion that you believed you deserved?

    _____

    _____

    _____

    _____

8. Tell me how pride and anger are related? _____

    _____

    _____

    _____

    _____

9. How does practicing forgiveness enable you to overcome bitterness? (Read Ephesians 4:32 and the passage that follows it.)

    _____

    _____

    _____

10. How does dealing with pride and anger properly help to free you from the likelihood of returning to addiction?

_____

_____

_____

_____

Notes:

Godly Wisdom for Self-discipline & Developing Friendships

Lesson 11

Name: _____

1. Is there any real Christian growth without self-discipline?

   _____

God is the initiator; we are the responder. What is our role as we grow in our relationship with Him?

_____

_____

2. What can you learn from Abraham's example as it is described in Hebrews 6:11-15? _____

   _____

   _____

3. II Peter 3:14-15 encourages us to be diligent in our walk with Jesus. How does our understanding of heavenly rewards affect our diligence today? _____

   _____

   _____

4. Describe the promises that God has for the diligent in Proverbs 10:4 and Proverbs 22:29.

   _____

   _____

5. What was Coach Dungy's philosophy?

   _____

How does this relate to God's call for us to be diligent in this life?

_____

_____

Relate it to the call in Colossians 3:22-25. _____

_____

_____

6. The Bible teaches that friendship is a good thing; however, it also
    warns that too many friends can actually be a problem. How can this
    be? _____

_____

_____

Have you ever experienced this? _____

7. There are five scripture passages in this chapter that counsel us on
    how to choose good friends. Based upon these passages, who should
    you avoid and who should you seek as friends?

_____

_____

_____

Are you permitting any on the negative list to influence you today?

_____

_____

_____

8. "Do not be unequally yoked together with unbelievers." This state-
    ment describes friendships, business partnerships, marriage and more.

What practical advice can you take from this statement in II Corinthians 6:14?

_____

_____

_____

Does it mean that you should not have acquaintances who are unbelievers? _____ How do you distinguish between "friends" and "acquaintances"?

_____

_____

9. How do you apply II Corinthians 6:14 when you are considering a marriage partner? _____

_____

_____

What does the Bible counsel you to do if you already married to someone who is not a Christian? (I Corinthians 7:10-15)

_____

_____

Notes:

The Eternal Construction Project

Lesson 12

Name: _____

1. The sign reads, "Caution: God (and men) at work." This is a message that Satan, your enemy, doesn't like to see. How have you seen him attempt to stop the work that the Lord has been doing in your life since you started *Beyond Addictions*?

   _____

   _____

   _____

2. Where does your real protection come from as you fight the battle against temptation and sin? _____

   _____

   _____

3. Why was Nehemiah discouraged when he heard about the condition of the wall around Jerusalem? _____

   _____

4. Compare the condition of the wall around Jerusalem with the conditions that you have seen in the lives of other men. Have you witnessed a time when you saw the walls of protection crumbling in someone else's life? _____ What did you see that caused you to be concerned? _____

   _____

_____

_____

5. What was Nehemiah's first response when he heard the news from Hanani?_____

What did he pray about? _____

_____

_____

6. Nehemiah told them the whole truth. Their lives were a mess and they were living in subjection to an enemy who wanted to destroy them. Are there any areas in your life where this is true? _____ If so, what are they? _____

_____

What do you need to do about them? _____

_____

7. Nehemiah also told them why the work would succeed. What did he say? _____

_____

8. The people responded with hope and said, "Let us rise up and build." You have also heard some good news that should encourage you. Which of the scripture passages quoted in this section mean the most to you right now? _____

_____

_____

9. Take Nehemiah 2:20 personally. What does it mean when you tell Satan that he has no heritage or right or memorial in you anymore?

_____

_____

_____

Are there any areas in your life where you need to remove the "memorials" of your past life? _____

If so, what should you do about them? _____

_____

_____

_____

_____

Notes:

Continuing the Work of Jesus Christ

Lesson 13

Name: _____

1. How did Sanballat respond to the work that the Lord was doing in Jerusalem? _____

_____

_____

2. How does this relate to the enemy's response to the work that God has been doing in your life while you have been involved in this course? _____

_____

_____

3. How did Nehemiah respond to Sanballat's attacks? _____

_____

_____

4. Have you ever allowed the ridicule of the enemy to discourage you?

_____

If so, did the ridicule and discouragement continue to take place?

_____

What does this tell you about the tactics of the enemy?

_____

_____

5. What does it mean to "have a mind to work"? _____

_____

_____

How does this relate to the last lesson on self-discipline? _____

_____

6. How can confusion lead you back into sin? _____

_____

_____

_____

7. How did Nehemiah respond to the enemy's attempt to confuse the workers? _____

Tell me what you should do to set a watch against the enemy day and night?

_____

_____

8. At one point, the people of Israel experience a little temporary failure in their work. What happened?

_____

_____

Explain how applying Hebrews 12:1-2 will enable you to avoid the trouble that they faced. _____

_____

_____

9. In the past you may have thought that you were the only one affected by your negative decisions. That wasn't true then and it isn't true now. How will those closest to you be affected by your <u>positive</u> decisions? _____

_____

_____

How does this motivate you to continue walking with the Lord? _____

_____

_____

_____

10. How can you prepare for spiritual attacks that may come in the normal course of your day? _____

_____

_____

_____

Notes:

Completing the Good Work that He Has Begun In You

Lesson 14

Name: _____

1. After facing opposition from Sanballat and the other enemies of Isra-
    el, the people of Jerusalem almost destroyed the work that God was
    doing in their city. What happened? _____

_____

Have you ever experienced a time when selfishness almost destroyed the
work that the Lord was doing in your life? _____ If so, how?

_____

_____

_____

2. There are blessings in serving, in looking out for the needs of others
    rather than being concerned about ourselves first. Can you think of
    some scripture passages that encourage you to think of others rather
    than yourself or to seek to serve rather than seeking to be served?

_____

_____

_____

3. Sanballat and his followers tried an interesting approach to draw Ne-
    hemiah away from the work that he was doing in Jerusalem (page 4).
    What did he do? _____

_____

How can you apply this to your own life? _____

_____

_____

4. How should you respond to accusations regarding your past?

_____

_____

_____

_____

5. How was Nehemiah protected from the false counsel of the priest?

_____

_____

How can you be sure that the counsel you are given is godly?

_____

_____

6. What is necessary for you to continue building on the foundation that God is establishing in your life? _____

_____

_____

7. Compromise is a killer. Can you identify any areas of your life in which you need to be especially on guard against compromise?

_____

_____

_____

_____

8. We need to have a regular heart cleansing to be sure that we are not compromising our faith in Jesus Christ, to be sure that we are not allowing thoughts and activities back into our life that can lead us back into sin. How can you search your heart in order to be sure that you are not already compromising your faith in Jesus?

_____

_____

_____

_____

_____

Notes:

Putting It All To Work

Lesson 15

Name: _____

Congratulations! You stuck with us to the end of the course. You have finished well. We have a little more work to do in order for you to put it all to work.

1. You recall from chapter 2, the importance of being transformed by the renewal of your mind. What are you doing differently to be sure that you continue to be changed by renovating the way you think?

_____

_____

_____

2. Read James 1:14-15. How does this relate to your old problems with addiction? _____

_____

_____

You cannot prevent Satan from tempting, but what can you do to keep him from leading you into sin? _____

_____

_____

_____

3. Addiction is idolatry. How does this Biblical truth help you to recognize and address problems before they grow into idolatrous addictions? _____

4. How does growing closer to Jesus keep you free from addiction?

   _____

   _____

   _____

5. It is much easier to be free from addiction when you are abiding in Jesus. What can you do daily to continue abiding in Him?

   _____

   _____

   _____

6. How does applying II Corinthians 5:17 keep you free from addictions? _____

   _____

   _____

7. Practicing forgiveness keeps us free from bitterness and removes a hook that the enemy can use to lure us back into sin. How can you put Ephesians 4:32 to work in your life? _____

   _____

   _____

8. Just like Sanballat attacked Jerusalem, Satan attacks you once you commit to live for Jesus. So you need to make it clear that Satan has no inheritance or right or memorial in your life anymore. Has the Lord been speaking to you about anything that you need to part with

(old habits, possessions or relationships) in order to be free from the temptations of the enemy? _____

_____

_____

9. What motivates you to be sure that you do not give in to compromise in your relationship with Jesus? _____

_____

_____

But, beloved, we are confident of better things concerning you, yes, things that accompany salvation, though we speak in this manner. For God is not unjust to forget your work and labor of love which you have shown toward His name, in that you have ministered to the saints, and do minister. And we desire that each one of you show the same diligence to the full assurance of hope until the end, that you do not become sluggish, but imitate those who through faith and patience inherit the promises. Hebrews 6:9-12

Therefore we also, since we are surrounded by so great a cloud of witnesses, let us lay aside every weight, and the sin which so easily ensnares us, and let us run with endurance the race that is set before us, 2 looking unto Jesus, the author and finisher of our faith, who for the joy that was set before Him endured the cross, despising the shame, and has sat down at the right hand of the throne of God. Hebrews 12:1-2

Continue growing in your faith.

Separate yourself unto Jesus

and He will separate you from addiction.

BIBLIOGRAPHY

Boa, Kenneth. *Conformed to His Image*. Grand Rapids: Zondervan, 2001. www.kenboa.org.

Broger, John C. *Self-Confrontation: A Manual for In-Depth Biblical Discipleship*. Palm Desert: Biblical Counseling Foundation, 1991. www.bcfministries.org.

Henry, Matthew. *Matthew Henry Commentary on the Whole Bible*. Christian Classics Ethereal Library. www.ccel.org/ccel/henry/mhc.i.html.

Hession, Roy. *We Would See Jesus*. England: The Roy Hession Book Trust, 1958. www.christianissues.biz/pdf-bin/sanctification/wewouldseejesus.pdf.

Hocking, David. *Proverbs for Today*. Orange, CA: Promise Publishing Co., 1991. www.davidhocking.org.

Thrasher, Bill. *A Journey to Victorious Praying*. Chicago: Moody Publishers, 2003.

Tozer, A.W. *This World: Playground or Battleground*. Camp Hill: Christian Publications, 1989.www.echurchdepot.com.

Tozer, A.W. *Whatever Happened to Worship*. Camp Hill: Christian Publications, 1985.www.echurchdepot.com.

Welch, Edward T. *Addictions: A Banquet in the Grave*. Phillipsburg: P&R Publishing, 2001. www.ccef.org.

Young, Sarah, *Jesus Calling*, Nashville, TN, Thomas Nelson, Inc., 2004

About the Author

Jeff Rudd is Director of Free In Christ Prison Ministries and an Assistant Pastor of Calvary Chapel of Cary, NC. Jeff began serving as a prison volunteer in 1994 while working as an economic developer, and later as a county manager in local government. In 2001, the Lord led Jeff to devote himself full-time to discipling prison inmates.

Jeff currently serves as a volunteer chaplain in two prisons. Over the past ten years, he has counseled more than 2,000 men, and taught more than 1,500 Biblically-based classes in prison. In addition to *Beyond Addictions*, he also teaches weekly Bible Studies, a course on how to understand and apply the Bible, and another to disciple men as Godly fathers. His approach is Biblical and practical as he enables men to apply God's Word to the issues they face in their daily lives.

The *Beyond Addictions* course is taught personally in two North Carolina prisons and it is available via correspondence or through other ministries in many other state prison systems. Hundreds of men have graduated from this course and gone on to lead productive lives in their communities. Many are using this course to disciple others who have struggled with addiction.

Jeff and his wife Deb are the parents of two sons, two daughters, and one very special daughter-in-law. They live in central North Carolina.

For more information on Free In Christ Prison Ministries, visit their website at www.ficpm.com or contact Jeff by snail mail at:

Jeff Rudd
Free In Christ Prison Ministries
PO Box 1492
Yanceyville, NC 27379
freeinchrist@esinc.net
www.ficpm.com